Mary Queen of Scots

CAROL SCHAEFER

Mary Queen of Scots

A Crossroad 8th Avenue Book
The Crossroad Publishing Company
New York

To my wonderful parents, G. Walker Kirby and Anne Neff Kirby
With love and gratitude.
And to my ancestors.

The Crossroad Publishing Company
481 Eighth Avenue, Suite 1550
New York, NY 10001

First published in 2002 by The Crossroad Publishing Company

Copyright © 2002 by Carol Schaefer

LIBRARY OF CONGRESS CATALOGING-IN-PUBLICATION DATA
Schaefer, Carol
Mary Queen of Scots / Carol Schaefer.
p. cm.
Includes bibliographical references and index.
ISBN 0-8245-1947-7 (alk. paper)
1. Mary, Queen of Scots, 1542–1587.   2. Scotland—History—Mary
Stuart, 1542–1567.   3. Great Britian—History—Elizabeth,
1558–1603.   4. Queens—Scotland—Biography.
I. Title.
DA787.A1 S33   2002
941'105'092—dc21
2002000654

Printed in the United States of America
Set in Janson
Designed and produced by SCRIBES Editorial

1 2 3 4 5 6 7 8 9 10 04 03 02

CONTENTS

Mary Queen of Scots

Clouet, Francois. (Follower of) Mary Queen of Scots.
(Victoria & Albert Museum, London/Art Resource, NY)

1

In My End Is My Beginning

The dark night of the soul comes just before revelation.
When everything is lost, and all seems darkness,
then comes the new life and all that is needed.

—*Joseph Campbell*

ON SUNDAY, JANUARY 29, 1587, between the hours of midnight and one o'clock, a great flame suddenly shone in the heavens and illuminated the window of Mary Stuart, queen of Scots' prison room, in the ancient castle of Fotheringhay in England. It was a great light and returned three times to the same place. In no other part of the castle could it be seen. This light was said to be so bright that one could easily have read or written by it. The guards who were appointed to watch under the queen's window were greatly astonished and alarmed. Did this light flood the queen's room and awaken her? Did Mary go in awe to the window and allow this other-worldly light to illuminate her? Was she suddenly flooded with solace, understanding now that the heavens also knew her end was near?

Ten days later, in the early morning hours of February 8, 1587, the day of her execution, Queen Mary lay fully dressed on her bed without any attempt at sleep. Her beloved friend and servant, Jane Kennedy, thought she seemed to be "laughing with the angels." The queen of Scots had only learned of her imminent death a few hours before.

"Sinister noises disturbed the silence of the night. Ominous sounds of hammering from the Great Hall. In the intervals of silence, the measured tramp of troupes posted around the castle could be heard."[1]

Serene amid her servants' tears she prayed:

O my Lord and my God, I have trusted in Thee.
O my dear Jesus, now liberate me.
In shackle and chain, in torture and pain, I long for Thee.
In weakness and sighing, in kneeling and crying,
I adore and implore Thee to liberate me.

As daylight dawned on that cold and bitter morning, in the month that still keeps all of winter's fierce cold yet also holds a faint promise of spring, Mary was taken to the Great Hall of Fotheringhay. She was dressed in a black satin cloak, embroidered with black velvet and set with black acorn buttons of jet trimmed with purple. A white lace-edged veil flowed from the top of her head down her back to the ground. She wore Spanish leather shoes in black and her stockings were edged with silver. Her garters were of green silk. In her hand, she held a crucifix and prayer book, and two rosaries hung from her waist.

The hall was hung all in black velvet. A great fire roared in the huge Gothic fireplace. Three hundred spectators filled the hall. A large crowd surrounded the castle. Troops of horsemen kept them under control. Three steps led up to the stage. Mary listened with dignity to the commission for her execution. When the executioner fell to his knees and asked for her pardon, she replied: "I forgive you with all my heart, for now I hope you shall make an end of all my troubles."

While Mary stood before the block, her servants Jane Kennedy and Elizabeth Curl helped her undress. "During the disrobing of this Queen, she never altered her countenance, but smiling said, 'I never have had such grooms before to make me unready, nor ever took off my clothes before such company.'" Customarily, women of royalty went to their end, if their fate was that they be executed, wearing white. In scorn for her enemies, Mary stood stripped to her red petticoat with its red, long-sleeved satin bodice trimmed with lace—red, the color of martyrdom in the Catholic Church, the color associated with harlots, the color of the goddess in ancient times.

Her servant Jane Kennedy bound Mary's eyes with a white cloth embroidered in gold, selected by Mary the evening before. After bidding her servants not to cry, Mary stood alone on the stage and positioned her chin herself on the executioner's block. To ease her discomfort, she placed her hands under her chin. As this would hinder the fall of the blade, the executioner gently took her arms and held them behind her back. Her last words before the first stroke of the ax were: "Into Thy hands O Lord I commend my spirit."

The first blow missed her neck and split open the back of her head. Mary was heard to whisper "Sweet Jesus." Her head was nearly severed by the second blow. The remaining sinew was completely cut through by the third blow.

Legend has it that when her head toppled off the block her body began moving, terrifying all the witnesses. When the executioner held up her head for all to see, her head slipped from her wig and fell to the floor. Her own hair had turned white and she was nearly bald from her long imprisonment. Without her great spirit to animate it, her face was unrecognizable, withered now like a crone's. The lips remained moving for the next fifteen minutes.

When the executioner reached under her skirt to claim her garter, which was his prerogative, his heart must have stopped. Mary's little Skye terrier, Geddon, devoted companion during her last years in prison, came out from hiding under her voluminous skirts and refused to leave his dead mistress. He lay in the blood between her head and her body.

A few thistles scattered over a mound of green grass and a solitary mass of masonry are all that remain to mark the scene of Mary's last sufferings. Purple thistles, nicknamed Queen Mary's Tears, still grow on the site of her execution, and are found wherever Mary resided or was imprisoned, whether in Scotland or England.

One of the most particularly satisfied witnesses, Sir Amyas Paulet, had been Mary Queen of Scots' last jailer. He had taken great pleasure in taking down Mary's cloth of state, which had hung over her chair in all her prisons during the last twenty years. Embroidered on the cloth, which featured a phoenix rising from the flames, was her motto: En ma fin git ma commencement. (In my end is my beginning.)

2

Of Stuart Kings and Queens

The fates said to them be kings of talent, but not of talent enough;
kings of deep inarticulate people, in whose heart is kindled fire of heaven,
which shall be unintelligible and incredible to you.
Take these heroic qualities, this sort of gypsy black.
Let there run in your quick blood pruriency of appetite, a proud impatience—
alas! an unveracity, a heat, and a darkness and try to govern in a time
frought with momentous issues and far reaching consequences.
That, we have computed, will be tragedy enough for your country and you.

—*Thomas Carlyle*

December 1542.

As his queen labored to bring forth an heir, King James V, the seventh Stuart king of Scotland, lay dying of a broken heart at Falkland, his beloved palace that he was inspired to build by his deep appreciation for the French Renaissance. After learning of the devastating and demoralizing rout of his troops by the English at Solway Moss, during this harshest of winters, his will was completely gone, and he collapsed and refused to fight for his own life. Instead he turned his face to the wall and rarely spoke again.

Whether or not he willed his own death, he prophesied it. When asked by his servants where they would be spending Christmas, he replied, "I cannot tell: choose ye the place. But this I can tell you, on Yule day, you will be masterless and the realm without a king."

The promise of a new heir gave James V no hope for the future, but only reminded him of the double tragedy that had struck both him and his queen so recently. Of James V it was said that he "sowed his wild oats with ungrudging prodigality." He fathered seven children by his various mistresses, but none were entitled to succeed him to the throne. Finally, the longed-for heir, Prince James of Scotland, was born to the king and queen, in May 1540. Increasing their blessings, a second son, Robert, was born at Falkland, in April 1541. But two days later, little Robert was dead. And within days of Robert's death, the little Prince James was found dead at Holyrood. John Knox, radical leader of the Protestant Reformation, and his followers hailed the double tragedy as Divine vengeance for the king's impiety. Some suspected poison. Most likely, their deaths were the result of the tenuous chances most infants had of surviving childhood in the sixteenth century.

His queen, Marie de Guise, whose family recently had risen to great political prominence in France, had assured her husband that they were young and would have many more heirs. Despite the fact that Marie de Guise was a noble, clear-headed and magnanimous woman, James felt no real love for her. Royal marriages were political matches, and rarely developed into a union of love.

On December 8, the Feast Day of the Immaculate Conception, in Linlithgow, the old and stately golden palace of Scottish kings, a princess was born. The regal and traditional lying-in place of queens, the birthing room in Linlithgow was in the northwest corner of the castle and overlooked the loch, chock full of perch and various other fishes. By the light of the blazing fire in the arched stone fireplace and the beeswax candles flickering from the relentlessly bitter drafts, her mother the queen and her attendants gazed adoringly and with relief at seeing such perfection. The queen named the infant Mary, after herself and in honor of the feast day of the Virgin Mary on which she was born. Outside the birthing room, social and political forces were gathering momentum, welling up from deep within a collective crying out for change against papal domination—forces that would bring this beautiful and gifted baby girl inevitably to the scaffold.

Within the hour, the queen's messenger entered the king's chambers at Falkland. As James V listened to the news that his queen had been delivered of a daughter, he never once turned his face from the wall. But he could be heard to say plainly enough, "Is it even so? The devil take it! Adieu, farewell! It cam wie a lass; it'll gang wie a lass." Those were the last words he ever uttered.

The first lass he was referring to was Marjorie Bruce, daughter of the greatest and the legendary Scottish king, Robert the Bruce. Marjorie Bruce married Walter the Sixth High Steward of Scotland, a hereditary office created by King David I to manage the royal household. She gave birth to the first king of the Stewart (or Stuart) line, crowned Robert II in 1371. In his despair, James V could not imagine the Stuart line living on beyond his helpless infant daughter.

For the next six days, the nobles of the realm, clad in thick furs, their feet wrapped in animal skins, traveled through the ice and snow from the deathbed of their king at Falkland to Linlithgow, to swear their loyalty to the tiny infant. Facing these lords, whose only fealty was to themselves and to their ravenous desire for power, Marie de Guise instinctively gathered her formidable strength to become as fierce as a mother bear defending her little cub against all treachery. Rumor spread that the child was exceptionally frail and would not survive, giving cause for innumerable machinations among those who smelled opportunity.

On the sixth day, the king sighed his last breath. The tiny babe succeeded her father to the throne, which she was to find for the rest of her life to be so perilous. James V left his daughter a troubled realm. With no grace period to grieve his loss, Marie de Guise, a skilled diplomat and formidable politician, vowed to hold onto the throne for her daughter any way she could. Immediately, plans for the little queen's betrothal were heatedly discussed in the courts of Europe and in England.

At his desk, the young preacher John Knox dipped his quill in the inkwell and wrote, "All men lamented that the realm was left without a male to succeed." Vulnerable to outside rule with a female on the throne, the country could be swallowed up. Whomever their tiny queen would marry would become ruler and control Scotland's destiny. The flamboyant and relentless Henry VIII was determined it would be his son Edward, Prince of Wales, age five. Such a marriage would unite England and Scotland and ensure English dominance over its neighbor for a very long time, if not forever. Further, the alliance would strengthen his kingdom against all enemies, especially France and Spain. His plan was to have Mary reared in the English courts, so that there would never be any question of her loyalties. Within the Scottish nobility were others with their own plans and who feared Henry VIII.

On July 21, while the little queen was barely out of her cradle and still cutting her teeth, an army of seven thousand, gathered by cardinal-archbishop of St. Andrews, David Beaton, arrived at Linlithgow to retrieve their sovereign and bring her to Stirling Castle, considered the strongest fortress in Scotland. As the procession made its way up the ancient volcanic rock to Stirling, the castle Mary's father had elaborately refurbished, making it the jewel of the Scottish Renaissance, Beaton and his nobles openly defied Henry VIII and his bullying tactics.

Still feeling secure with the recently signed Treaty of Greenwich, which provided for the marriage of Edward and Mary, despite the added Scottish stipulation that she remain in her own country, Henry VIII arrogantly demanded that mother and child be separated, and that the child be raised by English caretakers. Marie de Guise could live in town and visit her daughter when the keepers of her daughter saw fit. But with Henry's hold over the Scottish weakening and in further defiance, Mary's coronation was clandestinely held on the ninth of September 1543, when she was only nine months old.

In solemn procession across the courtyard, her lord keeper, Lord Alexander Livingston, carried the little queen, still too young to walk, to the ancient Chapel Royal. Wearing a regal crimson velvet mantle with an ermine-trimmed train over a jewel-studded satin gown with long hanging sleeves, Mary was able to sit up by herself when she was gently placed on the throne set up by the altar. Cardinal Beaton stood ready to perform the ceremony. Lord Livingston hovered close by to catch her should she fall. One row of pews was taken up by Mary's other lord keepers. The rest of the pews were taken by the equally-powerful feudal nobility, who perceived the investiture of the little queen as a token formality. For the ceremony, the earl of Arran, her Scottish suitor, bore the crown; the earl of Lennox, her future father-in-law, bore the scepter of crystal and Scottish pearl and the earl of Argyll bore the three-foot long ornate gilded sword of state, which would be ritualistically girded to the baby queen's body. The English supporters, except for the English ambassador, Sir Ralph Sadler, did not even bother to attend.

Lord Livingston answered the Coronation Oath for her, as she vowed to protect and guide Scotland as its true queen, consecrated and chosen by God. Her heavy regal robes were loosened and she was anointed with holy oil on her tiny chest, back and the palms of her exquisite little hands, the beauty of which poets would one day praise, and the legend of which would one day foil escape from her first prison. It is easy to imagine a baby's sudden tears as the chill emanating from the ancient stones of the centuries-old chapel reached her suddenly exposed little body. For a brief moment were any hearts shattered with unexpected compassion for the enormous and dangerous responsibility placed on such delicate and feminine shoulders, enough to rethink the ludicrousness of a ruthless and insatiable drive for a power, so ultimately illusive and spiritually unfulfilling?

Within the Scottish crown of jewels and gold, and of the oldest royal heritage in Europe, now placed on the little queen's head, was enclosed the circlet of gold worn by her great ancestor Robert the Bruce on his helmet at the famous and triumphant Battle of Bannockburn, which finally won back for Scots their independence from England. Robert the Bruce, whose blood descent from the ancient royal Celtic house of King David I, the Celtic kings Malcolm IV and William I, and even into the further depths of time to King Kenneth MacAlpin of the original Celtic Dalriada, wanted nothing less after establishing Scotland's independence from England than to restore Scotland to a wholly Celtic kingdom. Bruce was coronated twice. The second coronation took place two days after the first, in which, in accordance with Celtic tradition, he was anointed monarch on the throne of Scone.

Thus, within the shadow of the Protestant Reformation in which the infant Mary was crowned was a far more ancient battle for the hearts and minds and souls of the citizens.

ALL KINGS AND QUEENS of Scotland traced their succession from the biblical kings of Judah, from the princes of Greater Scythia and from the pharaohs of ancient Egypt. Scotland is said to be named after Scotia, a princess of Egypt, who traveled from her native land and married an Irish king. This archaic lineage within the Celtic kingdoms of Scotland, Ireland and Wales, carried with it a vein to sacred, esoteric teachings, which were forced over time against heavy opposition to go underground in order to be preserved.

Ancient Greeks regarded the Scottish hills and glens—the oldest of old rocks of the earth's first land mass—as sacred domain. To the ancient world, Scotland was known as the "crown of the Holy Isles beyond the western sea," and as late as the fifth century in Greece as the "Winged Temple of the Sun." The Scottish royal legacy was hewn on the Stone of Destiny, the venerated relic of the Bethel Covenant (Genesis 28:18–22). In 586, this stone, known as Jacob's Pillow, had been carried to Ireland from Judah during the reign of High King Eochaid of Tara, and then onto Scotland. The roots of Scottish royalty are wholly Celtic.

In a ritual dating from a time well before recorded history, the Celtic kingdom of Scotland was built around what then came to be known as the famous Stone of Scone, located on sacred ground called the "Hill of Belief," now called Moot Hill. Seated on the stone at the top of the sacred hill, the new monarch was invested with the regalia of his office, including a rod and mantle, and wedded to the land, to the people he ruled and to the earth goddess herself. This tradition, the responsibility of the monarch for the land's fertility, a belief also held by the ancient Egyptians, was based on an esoteric teaching from the most archaic times.

Twenty-four hundred years before Queen Mary's time, Scotland's Celtic Druid priests and priestesses were of a very advanced culture. They knew that Saturn's cycle around the planet took approximately thirty years. For them, the earth was never flat. By the time Mary was crowned, Celtic wisdom, with roots even much deeper into time, was known and preserved only within a few secret societies. These ancient wisdom teachings concerned physics, sacred geometry, alchemy, geomancy, astrology and astronomy and explained the very depths of the nature of the Divine, revealing how all of humanity and all of nature are connected.

Woven within the single code of knowledge, philosophy, science and religion, which once flourished universally, was the wisdom aspect of the Divine Feminine. In Celtic society, women were held in high esteem and enjoyed status as priestesses, prophetesses and receptacles and conduits for royal bloodlines. Never would women have been considered to weaken the throne.

The Knights Templar—the largest and most influential of the secret societies, a monastic order and a society of warrior monks and soldier mystics dedicated to the preservation and unfolding of the ancient wisdom teachings—nearly became extinct during the time of the Inquisition when members were imprisoned, tortured, tried and executed. The pope officially dissolved the Order of the Temple in 1312. Robert the Bruce had been excommunicated the year before. It is now believed by many that the Knights Templar, upholders of the Celtic tradition, reemerged and aided Bruce in his great victory at Bannockburn, as he sought restoration of a wholly Celtic kingdom, which had been abruptly lost with the murder of King Alexander III in 1286. Without high principles to guide them, and cut off from the original teachings, the people developed instead many superstitions. To honor his lineage and his beliefs, Bruce requested that when he died his heart be removed, placed in a silver casket, and buried in the Church of the Holy Sepulcher in Jerusalem, the place most revered in the ancient wisdom teachings.

This thread of mysticism from her famous ancestor, Robert the Bruce, was obvious in Mary from a very early age, as if his circlet of gold within the crown of Scotland remained with her from the moment of her coronation, magnifying for the rest of her life her own innate spirituality.

3

The Scots' Betrayal

One day Kore happened to be picking poppies in a field near Eleusis
when a great chasm opened in the earth with a thundering sound.
Out came Hades driving his chariot of black horses.
In one swoop, he grabbed Kore and carried her off to the underworld.

—*J. F. Bierlein*

THAT WINTER OF QUEEN MARY'S first birthday, howling winds buf-
feted the ancient fortress of Stirling castle relentlessly. Set high atop
a volcanic crag, the royal palace of Stuart kings and now queens lay
at a narrow crossing of the Forth between the Highlands and the
Lowlands. Many of the most important battles in Scottish history
were fought in the fields below. Heavy mists often obscured the
enormous sky, hiding the vast formal gardens and the ice-covered
glens awaiting the bloom of heather. Within the thick palace walls of
Renaissance splendor, warmed by the enormous fireplaces, and surrounded by children (some of them Mary's half siblings by her
father's mistresses), by ladies-in-waiting and great numbers of help,
mother and daughter felt secure.

But, beyond the haven of the tiny queen's fortress, her country
was experiencing the full force of Henry VIII's pitiless wrath against
the Scot's betrayal in taking back the hand of their Mary from his
son, in effect ending plans for England's peaceful annexation of
Scotland, thus jeopardizing his country's own safety against France
and Spain.

Unable to penetrate Stirling Castle and capture the little queen, Henry ordered the ruthless destruction of Edinburgh. The burning of the city took two days. Before being stopped at the city's fortress castle, the English ravaged their way through the town. Many children were murdered along with their parents and many more were orphaned. Food storage was pillaged and supplies taken as booty. Those who survived starved amid the smoldering ruins of homes and businesses, churches and abbeys. No one came to their aid.

The English captured the Scottish merchant ships and took care to demolish the castle of Lord David Seton and destroy his gardens and orchards, reputed to be the most beautiful in all of Scotland. From one of the most distinguished and influential Scottish families and a member of the Knights Templar, Seton was held responsible for the release of Cardinal Beaton, orchestrater of the Scot's betrayal of England.

Entering the sanctuary of Holyrood Abbey, as if fighting a holy war, the English desecrated the royal burial place of the Stuarts. Mary's father's coffin was dragged from its tomb and defiled. This was the first siege of what was called Henry VIII's "Rough Wooing" for his son. One can only wonder at the fear that pierced the heart of the mother for her daughter.

Marie de Guise had once been on Henry VIII's list of possible wives. To illustrate how practically incestuous political marriages were, her second husband, James V had once considered marrying Catherine de' Medici, who ended up being their daughter Mary's first mother-in-law. When considering Marie de Guise, Henry VIII declared that he was a big man and needed a big wife. Marie's response was that, though her stature was large, her neck was little.

Although Scottish alliance with France—even with its implied loss of independence—would seem preferable to annihilation by the English, the Scottish people were being bled by the Catholic Church, and France was a Catholic country. Half the revenues of the whole kingdom went to support the papacy. Worn down by Henry VIII's brutal treatment, the people could no longer tolerate the injustice of supporting the idleness of monks and friars while "the blind, crooked, bed-ridden, widows, orphans and all other poor, so visited by the hand of God as may not work," were being neglected. Such discontent tilled the soil for promoters of the Reformation. The people were provided books and pamphlets along with fiery sermons advocating the new religion.

In March of 1546, a leading Protestant preacher with the kindest, most gentle of hearts, George Wishart, was burned to death in the front courtyard of St. Andrews, while Cardinal Beaton and his bishops watched from cushioned seats along the castle's walls. Three months later, lords from Fife, disguised as masons overhauling St. Andrews, broke into the room where Cardinal Beaton lay with his mistress Marion Ogilvy, and, at the point of their swords, asked him to repent of Wishart's death. They then murdered him and mutilated his body. At noon, hanging by an arm and a leg from the same cushioned vantage where he had watched Wishart die, the cardinal was displayed naked for all the people to see, his severed genitals stuffed in his mouth. His body was then pickled and stuffed in a barrel, and stowed in the castle's famous Bottle Dungeon, while his assassins held St. Andrews for over a year.

With such extreme escalation of hostilities, her alliance with the Catholics now obviously meant Marie de Guise and her daughter were in grave danger of their own lives. What could not be known was that the Guise and Lorraine families were only feigning to be a stronghold of the Catholic Church in Europe and defenders of the faith against the Reformation. Marie de Guise was raised within a family that fully embraced and, by the early sixteenth century, had become dedicated sponsors of the works of, European esotericism with its roots deep into ancient history and kept alive within the Knights Templar tradition. Resurgence of esoteric teachings occurred alongside the Renaissance in Europe. Francois I welcomed to France many Italian Renaissance artists, architects and designers, whose influence created the French Renaissance. Many of the great artists and designers embraced esotericism and applied the principles of sacred geometry to their work, not just of architecture, but now also poetry, sculpture, music, and particularly theater. Leonardo da Vinci was one of these artists. He died in the arms of Francois I.

In the esoteric tradition, sacred geometry was a manifestation of the Divine. For instance, to master craftsmen, initiated in the sacred wisdom teachings, "a cathedral was more than a house of God. It was akin to a musical instrument tuned to a particular and exalted spiritual pitch, like a harp. If the instrument were tuned correctly, God Himself would resonate through it, and His immanence would be felt by all who entered." This union with the Divine was the sole purpose of applying esoteric knowledge to any of the arts.

Motivation for the enormous ambition of the Guise and Lorraine families—matrilineal ancestors of Mary Queen of Scots—to gain the French throne and to gain enough power to supplant or subsume the papacy, did not come solely from a ravenous desire for power, but to have the power needed to apply esoteric teachings on a large scale.

By way of Marie de Guise's marriage to James V, and through such families as the Stuarts, Setons, Hamiltons, Montgomeries and Sinclairs, and via the Scots Guard, esoteric thought was carried back to Scotland. A letter from Marie de Guise to Sir William Sinclair validates this little-known fact: "We bind us to the said Sir William, in likwis that we sall be leill and true maistres to him, his counseil and secret shewen to us we sall keip secret."

Held so strongly by her family and those who surrounded her in the French court growing up, these teachings, though not a religion, had to have been a part of Mary Queen of Scots' upbringing from the very beginnings of her life, and a great influence on her developing character and especially her innate mysticism.

A GESTURE FAR AHEAD of its time (or for that matter even ahead of ours today), her mother's gathering together of her daughter's "bastard" half siblings was a great benefit to Mary, who loved being a part of a large family. The oldest, then-fifteen James Stuart, who would have been king had he been legitimate, played a huge role in Mary's life for much of her life. James was stern and grave, and being much older, he was always deferred to by Mary and the other children.

Besides the half siblings, there were the famous "Four Maries" of legend and song: young girls, companions, ladies-in-waiting to the little queen, selected by Marie de Guise from families with close connections both to the royal house of Stuart and with France. From an early age, their personalities were distinctive.

The most flamboyant was Mary Fleming, nicknamed "La Flamina" because of her fiery disposition and strong personality. Older than the others, she was thought of as the "flower of the flock." La Flamina was the only one who could outdo the little queen's sense of fun and mischief. She and Mary shared the same grandfather, King James IV, so she, too, was of royal blood. Only Mary Fleming had a Scottish mother. The other three Maries, like their little queen, had French mothers and Scottish fathers.

Very robust and athletic, Mary Livingston was nicknamed "Lusty." Lusty enjoyed what would become Mary's lifelong passion for riding and for sport. When she was only three, Mary was presented with a little pony from the northernmost part of Scotland and began her riding lessons alongside Lusty.

Tall and stately, Mary Seton was known by her surname of Seton, one of the most illustrious of Scottish families. Mary Seton's father and grandfather were much involved with the Knights Templar. Various Seton homes became refuges for Mary Queen of Scots at different times in her life, and Mary Seton was the only one of the four never to marry. She stayed with her queen throughout her entire life.

Called Beaton to rhyme with Seton and make a pair, Mary Beaton was plump and pretty, and was often found swept up in a daydream. Beaton was a huge and powerful clan in Scotland in the sixteenth century. The murdered cardinal was a member of Mary Beaton's clan.

The children played together and grew closer and closer, little princes and princesses in a fairy tale, oblivious to the terrible monsters lurking just outside the castle walls.

IN THE MEANTIME, after believing herself for the past ten years to be barren, Catherine de' Medici, of the Italian family so instrumental in fostering the Italian Renaissance, gave birth to an heir to the French throne. Born a year after Mary during a solar eclipse—considered a powerful omen—Francois II's birth completely changed Mary's fortunes. But it took several other events to solidify the direction her life would take.

In January of 1547, Henry VIII died and his son Edward, age nine, succeeded him to the throne. Even with Henry's death, the pounding of the Scottish people by the English continued ferociously. In the spring, Francois I died and his son, Henry II, husband of Catherine de' Medici and father of Francois II, ascended to the French throne. On the tenth of September, the famous Battle of Pinkie Cleugh, a last-ditch effort by the Scottish people against the English, began, and turned into another debacle for the Scots. "The dead bodies lying about gave the impression of a thick herd of cattle, grazing in a newly replenished pasture."[1] One of the dead was Mary Fleming's father. The young girl had now lost all of her relatives, except her mother, in battles with the English. Her queen could sympathize, having never known her own father, because of his heartbreaking ruin at Solway Moss, or her grandfather, who died in the Battle of Flodden. As a result of the loss at Pinkie Cleugh, in combination with the great loss at Solway Moss five years before, there remained few fighting men left to prevent the English pillage of the countryside which followed.

The innocent cause of such relentless slaughter was now four and a half years old. Stirling Castle was no longer trusted to be unassailable while the English continued their wave of destruction close by, and the little queen was moved for three weeks to the enchanting and sequestered island of Inchmahone, home to an exquisite priory run, since the thirteenth century, by monks of the Augustinian Order. The island's romantic setting, with its views of the mountains, combined with the little queen's own special magic and poignant vulnerability to create quite a few delightful legends about her brief stay there. Honoring her on the island today are the centuries-old Queen Mary's Garden, Queen Mary's Bower and Queen Mary's Tree, which still draw worshiping tourists.

It is easy to imagine that such a sudden and clandestine trip made a deep impression on Mary. The beauty of the island, the ritual, the prayers and chanting of the monks and the sacredness of the place must have softened her young psyche to her own spirituality.

WITHIN THREE WEEKS, the English were gone and the royal entourage returned to Stirling for the winter. Safe again for a little while, the children were allowed outside to play, and often sledded down the ice-covered hill behind the castle using a cow's skull. In February, they moved to Dumbarton Castle on the west coast of Scotland.

An alliance with the French was now the only thing that made sense for Scotland. But as the betrothal of Mary to Francois, the dauphin of France, was being debated in Parliament, Mary became deathly ill. Rumors spread that she had in fact died, and the fragility of foreign policy resting on such young shoulders was obvious. But Mary survived what seemed to be nothing more than an attack of the measles, and in July 1948, when she was five and a half years old and her prospective bridegroom was four, their marriage was approved by Parliament—with the provision that France agree to protect Scotland, while, at the same time, respecting completely Scotland's independence.

The violence rampant in the country by the English against the Scots and by the country's own savage way of dealing with religious and political conflicts, prevented the common people from ever actually seeing their little queen; this may have created the foundation of mystery for her legendary status. Nevertheless, word of Mary's beauty and charm seeped from the castle walls like gossamer, keeping the magic of Scotland alive. One Frenchman paying a visit to the little queen exclaimed she was the most perfect creature he had ever seen. With such splendid beginnings, he felt anything could be expected of her. "It is not possible to hope for more from a Princess on this earth," he proclaimed.

Ultimately, however, with all its violence and bloodshed, Scotland lost its innocent and gifted child-queen to a country with greater ability to nurture her very special spirit.

4

Her Simple Glance

The tongue of Hercules, so fables tell,
All people drew by triple chains of steel.
Her simple glance where 'er its magic fell,
Made men her slaves, though none the shackles feel.

—*M. du Bellay*

PERCHED HIGH ABOVE THE gray and choppy waters of the Firth of Clyde, the stronghold of Dumbarton Castle appeared from the royal galley—sent by Henry II to retrieve his son's betrothed—to be clinging to the rock. Boarding the galley to accompany the now almost six-year-old Scottish queen on her trip to France and protected by the Scots Guard, was an entourage of lords and ladies and children, including several of her siblings and the Four Maries. Loaded for the trip were gifts, including Shetland ponies for the young French prince and princesses and the other children of the royal French nursery. All boarded the ship except Mary's beloved mother, who was to stay behind and protect the Scottish throne.

Desperate with sorrow, Marie de Guise watched as the sails of the great galley took hold of the blustery wind and carried her daughter away from the important western seaport of Scotland, and onto the treacherous journey to her new life. Life in Scotland had become more perilous for the little queen than the dangerous journey ahead. Fear that the galleys would be intercepted by the English was real enough that the decision was made to travel the longer western route rather than the shorter route from the eastern coast. While the English proved to be no threat, fierce storms caused everyone on board, except Mary, to become violently ill. Caught up in the thrill of the adventure, Mary's spirits were high and she never became seasick, despite the turmoil of the sea. Instead, she had fun teasing the others over their maladies.

Off the Cornish coast, the wild waves were so huge from the gales that the ship's rudder was smashed. According to one Frenchman's account, only Divine intervention enabled them to quickly repair the rudder and prevent disaster. Mary never once expressed any fears. Still chased by storms, the captain was unable to come even close to landing on the western coast of France for several days. Finally, a spot was found on a rocky protrusion, of the small village of Roscoff, the hub of much activity by pirates and smugglers.

The huge and badly battered galleys set anchor and rowboats were lowered into the water. It was the thirteenth of August 1548. Along the shore, townspeople gathered, drawn in wonder by the dramatic sight of the wounded but still elegant ships. The little queen of Scots was on the first boat to row to shore. Legends immediately sprang up around the small town as soon as the child-queen put her first footstep on French soil there.

Leaving behind a mostly barren-looking and treeless country of rugged people forever having to defend their land, and on her way to the most brilliant court in the world, Mary and her entourage passed through peaceful, pastoral scenes of thatched roof farmhouses and the prosperous villages of Normandy. Local dignitaries along the way welcomed them and fed them well. The trip to the French court took two months.

In Morlaix, at the very beginning of the journey, Mary was received by the lord of Rohan and much of the nobility of the nearby countryside. Her lodgings were a Dominican convent. During her stay, a Te Deum was sung in thanksgiving for her safe arrival. To the embarrassment of the local welcoming committee, on their way out of town the local drawbridge broke and fell into the river under the weight of the horsemen. The suspicious Scottish lords in the party shouted, "Treachery!" Lord Rohan shouted back indignantly, "No Breton was ever a traitor!" To pacify the wary Scots, the chains of the bridges in the town were broken and all the gates were taken off their hinges until Mary and her party left.

When Mary's entourage reached the Seine, a gorgeously decorated and luxurious barge, sent by the king, awaited to take them on the last part of their journey. They slept in beds with sumptuous linen and headboards decorated with gold leaf. Privy stool-closets were hung with crimson velvet and kept fresh with vases of irises. They drank from crystal goblets and ate from plates of gold. On their way to the royal Chateau of St. Germain-en-Laye, they traveled upriver though the beautiful valley of the Loire. Wherever Queen Mary passed on her way from Roscoff to St. Germain, prison gates opened and pardoned criminals were released. Honors and rejoicing met her all along the way.

Even at such a young age, Mary was said to be genuinely interested and kind to all. "Whenever she addressed anyone, she had a very sweet, fascinating and pretty yet dignified, way of speaking, and with a discreet and modest sort of familiarity and gentle gracefulness. She had, too, this special perfection to enchant the world."[1]

Mary possessed a rare beauty, even as a child, which came as much from her spirit as from her physical features, and proved difficult for the artist to capture on canvas. Her naturally golden hair framed a broad brow, a lofty forehead and accentuated her unusually white skin. Her eyes, clear and searching, ingenuous, sometimes hazel, sometimes chestnut, were always direct, unflinching and as fearless as a hawk's. Her eyelids were unusually heavy with an uninterrupted curve. Her face was pure in its sweetness, simplicity and sedate composure. Her expression even when young was grave. There was a wistfulness that always played about it, as if she somehow already knew her fate. Apart from the grave composure and wistful pensiveness, it was a somewhat ambiguous face, changing always with her mood. But it was a powerful and captivating face, nevertheless, with a sedateness older than her years, and a smile that, when the gravity gave way, is said to have rivaled the sun in its radiance.

FROM HER FIRST FOOTSTEP onto French soil, Mary instantly became a romantic creature and a heroine in the eyes of the French: a brave little queen, forced to flee a barbaric country and the perpetual threat and bullying of the English; an orphan of sorts, her mother poignantly left behind in an uncivilized and untamed country. Her new country instinctively embraced her, wanting to nurture her, and fell completely in love.

On her journey to the court, Mary met the woman who, during her youth in France, was to have the strongest influence on her developing character. Her grandmother, Antoinette de Bourbon, duchesse de Guise, joined the travelers midway to prepare Mary for all she was to experience when she reached the court.

Upon meeting her granddaughter for the first time, Antoinette wrote to her daughter, Marie: "I pity the sorrow that I think you must have felt during her voyage, and I hope you had news of her safe arrival, and also the pain that her departure must have caused you. You have so little joy in the world, and pain and trouble have been so often your lot, that methinks you hardly know now what pleasure means." Her letter went on to console and reassure her daughter that her loss also meant her daughter's safety. Thrilled with her granddaughter, she promised Marie she would do all she could to ensure Mary would make a grand impression on the court, and especially on her future in-laws, the king and queen of France.

The first order of business would have to be an immediate overhaul of her wardrobe. Scottish tastes were far, far below the elegant refinement of the French. Mary needed some quick polishing up, and perhaps less time with her less cultivated Scottish companions. As for herself, the duchesse was "a lady of stainless repute," who always wore the simplest of gowns, and often appeared at court in gowns of black serge. Married to Claude, duke of Guise, when she was sixteen, Antoinette gave birth to twelve children, ten of whom not only survived but, so unusual in those days, thrived.

A story about how she dealt with her husband's infidelity with a local village girl reveals facets of her towering nature: her confidence, her managerial ability and her sense of humor. The trysting place was a tiny hut on the edge of their vast estate. Without a word about her knowledge of his infidelity, Antoinette asked her husband to meet her at the very same hut, called La Viergeotte. To her husband's great surprise, Antoinette had completely redecorated the hut and transformed it into a nest of lavish pleasure, only now worthy of her husband. More pleasure and surprises must have awaited him, for, afterward, Duke Claude built a small castle on the spot, with the interlacing letters A and C prominent, and with the words, "All for one; and no other" inscribed.

While trappings of the court meant nothing to her, she had enormous pride and ambition where her children were concerned. As a young mother, she was convinced of their destiny to play a large role in the world. Whether, when they were children, she saw into their future, or with her ambition created in them the drive necessary, or both, the Guise children did exert a great deal of power in the world. And this little granddaughter promised to ensure enduring influence and greater and greater power for the family for a very long time.

ANTOINETTE WAS CONFIDENT of her granddaughter's preparation by the time the standard for the royal house of Valois could be seen flapping in the light breeze, and the barge drifted into the landing for St. Germain-en-Laye. This magical world that Mary was entering, a world devoted to pleasure, poetry, art, architecture, cuisine, music, dance and beauty, was the peak of the French Renaissance and the finest epoch of French taste. Henry's court continued the brilliance and sophistication of his father, Francois I, who patronized as many artists, philosophers and scholars as he could. The court embodied an exquisite delicacy: a simplicity, a refinement of detail, a studied elegance. Gowns were luscious. Knitted silk stockings for men were like a second skin. Caps were worn at an angle, feather always upright.

At the same time that it was voluptuous, the court was also steeped in ennui, and discontent pervaded. Perfect conformity of sentiment and taste were required, and there was no more room for individual expression than in a monastic community. Restrained by impeccable refinement to laugh without gaiety, dance and revel without inclination, everyday life at the court was as restrictive as a religious fast or vigil.

As rigid in his own thinking as the restricted manners awaiting Mary, the Scottish Protestant Reformation preacher, John Knox, predicted that having spent her youth in the French court, "she should drynk of that lycour, that should remane with her all her life-time, for a plague to this realme, and for her finall destructioun." These were ironically righteous words given that at least Mary had an excellent chance of staying alive in France, where in her own country, the discontent and violent measures of John Knox and his followers would surely have meant a short life for the little girl.

The king and queen were not there to greet her (Henry was on campaign in Italy), but the children of the royal nursery, including Francois, her little betrothed, and his two younger sisters soon arrived. The king's mistress, the legendary Diane de Poitiers, who fashioned herself after the moon goddess Diana, was the one responsible for making all feel welcome and at home.

Although already forty-eight years old when she greeted the Scottish entourage, Diane de Poitiers completely captivated and fascinated her royal lover until the end of his life. Her beauty only increased with age, and she was blessed with great intelligence, health and an abundance of energy. She was a Renaissance mistress, not a kept plaything, and involved herself in the arts and in every aspect of her lover's kingdom, caring for his family as if they were her own. That care and concern included fostering his relations with his wife, the queen, Catherine de' Medici. Married at fifteen, Diane de Poitiers raised two successful daughters of her own, and many in France could not handle her flagrant adultery with the king, or reconcile it with her ability to raise respectable daughters. Many in Scotland believed the poor choices made by Mary Queen of Scots in her adult years were a direct result of being debauched by the influence of the king's mistress. It is not hard to imagine that her fanciful beauty and magic could have held Mary spellbound, as if this fairy godmother-like creature were from some exotic fable.

There must have been much anxiety felt by everyone about whether Francois, nearly five, and Mary almost six, would get along. Francois had an affectionate disposition, but took little pleasure in the company of others, even at a young age. He was shy and timid and shrank from the responsibilities of his rank and station. But from the moment they met, the two became excellent friends. They were observed going "to the end of the room by themselves to exchange apart from the others their little confidences." In the presence of his spirited and charming intended bride, Francois' frigidity vanished.

In contrast to Mary's captivating beauty, Francois was homely, nothing to please the eye. "Owing to an unfortunate nasal obstruction, he could not speak without offending the ear. Feeble limbs and a low stature gave him a meanness of appearance and an insignificance, which was not redeemed by intellectual gifts."[2] Nurses and physicians attended him from the cradle. In no way was he a match for his bride. Still, Mary loved him instantly and without reservation, and Francois followed her from then on like an adoring shadow.

"The fact of their superiority and power was forever kept before the eyes of infant royalties, and crushed all youthful spontaneity long before they reached adolescence. Mary's strong natural character and marked individuality kept her from becoming a prig."[3] But the training she would receive did contribute to her lifelong pride and sense of sacred sovereignty. Before she left the nursery, she would learn to "enact the pageant of the future queen. A certain step and carriage were among the chief requisites."

A MONTH FULL OF adventure and much learning, especially of the customs and the language, passed before the king and queen arrived at St. Germain. As always, the king arrived with a retinue of at least 12,000 horses; his retinue in times of peace could be as many as 18,000 horses. "The little Queen of Scots is the most perfect child that I have ever seen," he declared. And the queen Catherine de' Medici commented that, "This small Queen of Scots has only to smile in order to turn all French heads."

With their parents' unlimited resources and enormous devotion and solicitude, it is possible that the children of Henry II and Catherine de' Medici were the most lavished of children in all of history. A mother above anything, Catherine de' Medici was nearly deprived of the one role she craved more than anything else. Not of royal blood and therefore forever looked down upon, and with no great beauty or charm as antidotes, Catherine's marriage to the French king was a result of her famous Italian family's dowry and their connections to the pope. Given Henry II's father's devotion to the arts, the Medicis' great role in bringing about the Italian Renaissance was probably another strong reason for the match.

During the first years of her marriage Catherine was sterile, unable to reach puberty. Rumors abounded that she was to be sent back to Italy. Given that the Medicis and much of the French court were immersed in esoteric thought, it is easy to imagine that Catherine employed every magical as well as medicinal art to her cure. Finally, in 1544, Francois was born, and a brood of six quickly followed. From the moment her first blessing was born, not a single minute detail regarding the care of any of her children (three others died at birth) weighed in any less importance in her mind than the most urgent matters of state.

Mary was equally bestowed with such total devotion. Actually, given she was a reigning queen, Henry ordered that Mary walk ahead of his own daughters and be treated with even greater deference. He wrote, "I want her to be honoured and served." When staying at court, Mary was to share a room with their oldest daughter Elizabeth. Henry wanted very much the two young girls to be friends. Presumably to cleanse her of all her less-than-civilized Scottish influences and prepare her for her role as future queen of France, Henry ordered that Mary be raised apart from her siblings and the Four Maries, who were sent to live in a convent of Dominican nuns in Poissy. Cut off from her cherished childhood friends, Mary became intimate friends with Elizabeth, two and a half years younger than herself. The next youngest sister, Claude, would also be her dearest friend.

Although when at the court, Mary was cocooned in an atmosphere of ultra-civilized luxury, protected from any contaminating influence, much of her youth was in fact spent in an atmosphere of austerity with her grandmother and her aunts, devoutly Catholic women, to whom the follies and frivolities of the court meant nothing. To remind herself on a daily basis of her mortality, Antoinette kept her own coffin in the gallery that led to the chapel, so that she could pass by it every day on her way to and from Mass.

Such an eccentric and dark ritual must have made a deep impression on her little granddaughter, as she followed her grandmother down the hall to Mass. As if meant to soften the blow of her own destiny, the memory of her grandmother's daily practice of facing death must have surfaced forty years later to give Mary the strength she needed to so calmly kneel and, without a tear, rest her head on the executioner's block.

5

The French Court

In jump rope rhymes, twentieth-century children chant,
"Mary Queen of Scots Got Her Head Chopped Off!"
—*Liz Lochhead*

FAIRY TALES OF KINGS AND QUEENS, princes and princesses, fantastic castles and magical lands have been part of growing up for most children throughout the ages. But how does a little queen or future king listen to such fables? Surely such tales were told in the royal French nursery. Nothing was ever spared them. The children were always surrounded by anything their hearts desired. Following them on their journeys from palace to palace were great numbers of pets of all kinds, including for a while two bears, until the cost of feeding them and repairing all the damage they caused became too great. Any sort of traveling troupe of entertainers of any kind of merit passing by was invited to perform. The slightest occasion was seized upon as cause for celebration and rejoicing. The spirit of fun and play was an essential part of each day for the pleasure-loving household.

Just as all young children naturally play house, so did little Francis and Mary. They loved each other so much, or else took their future roles so seriously, that people commented on how they already treated each other like sweethearts or husband and wife. King Henry, whose delight and tenderness toward Mary was obvious from the moment he first met her, wrote to Mary's uncle the duke of

Guise that Francis and Mary played so well and got along so beautifully it was as though they had known each other all their lives.

Living like opulent gypsies, the merry family moved every few months from one luxurious and magnificent palace to the next, all far grander than the grandest castle Mary had ever known in Scotland. The family followed the seasons and the hunt, and left each palace as soon as it needed cleaning. So, each few months, the children set out on new adventures to one of their lavish estates. Favorite of the children was Anet, the chateau of Diane de Poitiers. Inspired by the goddess Diana, the beautiful palace had a magical quality, and was the setting for much entertainment. What did Mary think about it all and about herself as she looked out from the carriage and saw the small peasant children her own age lined along the way, hoping to catch a glimpse of the little queen or a real live prince or princess?

Days at the court had a certain established routine. The king rose always at seven and held business meetings in his bedroom until just before ten in the morning. Mass was at ten. Marie de Guise emphatically stipulated that her daughter attend Mass daily. After Mass, the whole family spent time together for the next couple of hours, and then joined the lords and ladies of the court where religion, politics, love and intrigue all intermingled. The king appeared to enjoy Mary's company so much that he spent hours at a time talking with her. By the time Mary was eleven, the king could speak with her as if she were a woman of twenty-five. Over the years, she learned a great deal about all facets of ruling from their lengthy discussions.

Afternoons were spent with the royal chase, or either playing or watching tennis in the queen's garden. In the evenings, the ballet or music of some kind was offered, and twice a week there was a ball. Without singing and dancing, the royalty could not stay in good humor. Children were allowed to take part when they turned twelve.

Education during the Renaissance was secular rather than religious. Education for women became fashionable, especially in the courts of Francis I and Henry II. Languages were emphasized:

Latin, Greek and French in particular, but also Spanish, Italian and English. Mary became fluent in several languages, but all of her life preferred to use French as her primary language. Classical literature, Plato, Cicero and especially Plutarch were studied extensively. Erasmus was the only contemporary writer taught. Subjects ranged from philosophy and poetry to drawing and needlework, elocution, dancing, horsemanship and the hunt. Performing in masques and ballets delighted Mary, and she loved all outdoor activities. Music was also emphasized, and Mary sang with a rich, sweet voice, often accompanying herself on the lute, "with lovely hands, so finely fashioned that those of Aurora herself could not surpass them," in the words of the poet Brantome. Mary also learned to play the harpsichord and cithern.

Her writing mentor was the poet M. de Ronsard, founder of the Pleiades School, who praised Mary's poems, which she began writing when very young. They became lifelong friends. Along with Ronsard, the poets M. du Bellay, and M. de Maisonfleur wrote beautiful poems in praise of her. In her later years of imprisonment, she reread them with tears in her eyes and sorrow in her heart, as she recalled happier days. Mary's essays were written with force and passion and with her own unique devotional feeling. When she was ten, Mary delivered a Latin oration before the king and nobles about the importance of higher education for women. Her speech was delivered with "spirit and animation, which delighted the court." By nature, she was courteous and considerate, frank and sincere, able to win all hearts with her charm and grace of manner. She was a bright, lively, intelligent child, but could also be grave and reserved.

"There was a strong mystical vein in her nature . . . she was an apt and willing scholar and had the love of learning for its own sake, which is very uncommon."[1] When studying at the convent during her early years, she never minded the ascetic life of her grandmother, who tried to guard her from the easy morals of the court, and supervised her moral training, wanting her to "serve God well and live virtuously." In fact, Mary responded so intensely to her spiritual teachers that they hoped she would adopt a religious vocation.

From her far distant homeland, Mary's mother was in constant contact with those in Mary's charge, and not even the slightest detail of her daughter's upbringing was unimportant. Uppermost was her daughter's religious education. When, at the age of seven, it came time for her to receive the sacrament of Holy Communion, Mary wrote to her mother to request her permission, expressing her fervent desire to "receive God," and signing her letter, "Your very humble and obedient daughter, Marie."

Mary had two chaplains of her own, a French priest and the prior of Inchmahone, who out of complete devotion, and asking no wages, stayed with Mary and served her from the time she visited his beautiful monastery as a little five-year-old. The frequent and often florid praise of the young queen of Scots would be expected from a court steeped in extravagance of any kind. It is impossible to find an unkind word about her from anyone who knew her during her years in France. But where it would be understandable that so much praise was the result of her role in the court, with probable fears of repercussions for any negative comments, the prior of Inchmahone's selfless devotion to the young girl's soul may be a clue that there really was something extraordinary about Mary Stuart, and the praise heaped on her by so many was in fact deserved.

Longing to see her daughter and a son Francis, by her first marriage, and feeling increasingly depressed and isolated in Scotland, Marie de Guise set sail for a visit to France. Two years had passed since Mary last saw her mother, and the impact of their separation on the seven and a half-year-old's developing character is apparent from a very telling letter she wrote her grandmother, informing her of the impending visit:

Madame, I have been very glad to be able to send these present lines, for the purpose of telling you the joyful news I have received from the Queen, my Mother, who has promised me by her letters dated April 23 that she will be here very soon to see you and me, which is to me the greatest happiness which I could wish for in this world, and indeed I am so overjoyed about it, that all I am thinking about now is to do my whole duty in all things and to study to be very good, in order to satisfy her desire to see in me all that you or she hope for . . .

When her mother arrived in September of 1550, Mary's preparation for her visit was obvious. With utmost gravity, she inquired as to "whether any feuds continued to subsist in the noble families of Scotland," and if the "ancient faith" and "divine worship" were still followed, and did the English "still harass her dear native country."

Her eagerness to please her mother, who loomed larger than life in her imagination—a woman so strong as to rule Scotland and so devoted as to sacrifice all for her daughter's future—was also fueled by the powerful personalities of her uncles, especially Charles de Guise, cardinal of Lorraine. The formidable personalities of the Guise family members, combined with their high expectations for their young niece's role in strengthening an already strong power base, had to have created the precocious maturity so obviously a part of her personality. Understanding her role, practically from the cradle, Mary knew what she needed to do to please those she loved. Her naturally loving nature never needed to question, but only desired to fulfill their hopes and dreams.

WHERE TO MARY STUART, survival simply meant having to please others who were easily pleased, across the waters in England, to the young woman of seventeen who would one day give the orders for the now eight-year-old queen of Scots' execution, survival was literally a daily battle. In stark contrast to the indulgent French, child-rearing in England demanded slave-like obedience to parents. A precocious seriousness was required of children, who were expected to develop a modest and prim decorum. Whippings and beatings were thought to be essential. Henry VIII demanded blind obedience of his children, and the only one of his children whose spirit he did not eventually break was Elizabeth's.

"Probably no royal birth in English history was quite such a grievous disappointment as Elizabeth Tudor's."[2] Married to the Spanish princess Catherine of Aragon, widow of his older brother Arthur who had died unexpectedly five months after the marriage,

Henry came to believe his marriage had offended the Almighty Himself. Plagued by one miscarriage after another of Catherine's, his hopes of producing a male heir looked bleak. Stillbirths were considered a sign of God's displeasure, and since God had blessed him in every other way, it must be his wife who was the target of God's disfavor. Opening his Bible to the Book of Leviticus one early spring day in 1527, he read in the twentieth chapter: ". . . if a man shall take his brother's wife, it is an unclean thing. . . . They shall be childless."

Henry VIII's conscience was pricked. Sudden and untapped scruples came to the fore. Like a weed, his conviction grew that for eighteen years he had lived in incestuous adultery with his brother's wife. The incalculable ripple of the ensuing annulment affected the entire course of English history and consciousness.

For the six years before his "enlightenment," Anne Bolyn had resisted the king's advances and kept him enthralled. Her sister, Mary, had long been his mistress, and seeing how that got her sibling nowhere, Anne had no intention of going down the same unrewarding path. She went for the king with vision, courage and an amazing strength of will. According to one contemporary, "Madame Anne was not one of the handsomest women in the world; she was of middling stature, swarthy complexion, long neck, wide mouth, bosom not much raised, and in fact had nothing but the English king's great appetite and her eyes which were black and beautiful, and invited conversation." Her hair was glossy, thick and black, and she had a great deal of sexual magnetism. She was also known for her "venomous temper, rapacious ambition, and tendency toward hysteria."

Anne Bolyn finally gave in to the king's advances and became pregnant with what was thought to be Henry's longed-for male heir. A wedding date had to be set in haste. The queen Catherine of Aragon refused to consent to a divorce, preferring to be a poor woman begging for alms than be bribed. Defying the pope, insulting the European heads of state, and offending a huge proportion of his subjects—despite his seemingly unassailable popularity—an annulment was declared, the wedding date set and his excommunication assured. Few lined the streets to witness the queen's coronation.

"On September 7, 1533, the new queen was delivered of a girl, to the great disappointment and sorrow of the king, of the lady herself and of others of her party, and to the great shame and confusion of physicians, astrologers, wizards and witches, all of whom affirmed the baby would be a boy." Henry reacted with rage. He had risked everything: his throne, his soul and the safety of his kingdom. He saw Elizabeth as a great joke played on him by the Almighty. In defiance of the Almighty and everyone else, Elizabeth was flaunted, carried about in a sumptuous velvet litter, while his daughter by Catherine, Mary Tudor, was forced to walk beside her half sister or travel in a conspicuously plain conveyance, like an ordinary woman. Mary Tudor was humiliated, put to shame before the people of England, most of whom still held her as the rightful heir. It is understandable that Elizabeth could never embrace Catholicism or even tolerate it, when her very birth defied the pope.

Rumors flew about the court that Anne Bolyn was a whore and had had over a hundred lovers, and that Henry was in fact impotent. Condemned as an adulteress and a traitor when Elizabeth turned two and a half, Anne Bolyn publicly pleaded to Henry, who stood in the courtyard below her window, to spare her life for her beloved daughter's sake. She never believed he would put her to death. But when it became clear that Henry would not relent, she said she was ready to "yield herself humbly to the will of the king." She laid aside the furred mantel of her gray gown and crushing her bountiful black hair under a plain linen cap, bared her long white neck to the executioner's sword. The executioner finished his task with one stroke, and Anne Bolyn's head was wrapped in a white cloth. "Old women who charmed herbs and cast spells crowded to the scaffold to catch drops of Anne Bolyn's blood, for the blood of the condemned was said to be especially potent." Her headless body was stuffed into a crude coffin and buried, without ceremony, in St. Peter's Church.

Masses of black hair. Dark and bewitching eyes. A scent. A lingering lullaby. A fierce protectiveness of both their lives. Haunting wisps of nurturing love. Could her mother's ghost ever be laid to rest? No longer with anyone's love to shield her, Elizabeth, even at a young age, must have known how her mother died, and that it was her father who ordered her execution. The backstabbing court of the time would have gleefully made her aware. How deep her unresolved grief must have gone to allow her, years later, to order another queen beheaded, one to whom she was related by blood, and one who, like her own mother, also left a child behind.

With her mother's death, Elizabeth was no longer a princess but considered a bastard like her half sister Mary. On top of that, she was the daughter of a condemned adulteress and traitor. From that point on, she was raised almost like a pauper, literally wearing rags for clothes. When Elizabeth was four, her father's next wife, Jane Seymore, gave birth to the longed-for male heir, Edward II, the son he hoped so much for the little queen of Scots to marry. In his relief, her father began to pay better attention to both daughters. When she turned nine, Elizabeth swore to her then-little friend and future great love, Robert Dudley, that she had made up her mind never to marry.

If Mary Stuart had been toughened by adversity, as Elizabeth clearly was throughout her growing up years, would she have been the one able to survive their looming rivalry? Mary Stuart had always been protected from the harsh realities around her. Even when loss and trouble came, she was surrounded by people who nurtured her through such hardships, putting the best possible spin on a situation to console her.

AFTER A YEAR OF BEING nearly inseparable, mother and daughter's love for each other only strengthened by knowing their time together was short. Thus Mary was able to bear her grief when her mother sailed back to Scotland. During her year in France Marie de Guise was frequently entertained by the court, which considered her daughter to be a little goddess. Marie de Guise's financial worries became an annoying subject to the crown, though, as she sought aid for her cause in Scotland. During her visit, there was a mysterious and frightening attempt on her daughter's life, but she did leave reassured that her daughter was being treated with utmost love and care, and that her daughter was becoming, in every way, all she could ever hope for.

At the same time that she lost her mother back to Scotland, Mary lost her cherished friend and governess from childhood, Lady Mary Fleming. The mother of La Flamina, one of the Four Maries, Lady Fleming had caught the king's eye from the time of her arrival in France. The king was bewitched by the pretty Scotswoman's high spirits, and they began a flagrant affair. A son was born as a result, who became known as the Bastard of Angouleme. Lady Fleming's happiness and the naïve honor she felt bearing a child of the king's would have to be enough to sustain her. Even the king's own desires were no match for the wrath of the other two women who shared his bed, and the pregnant Lady Fleming was immediately shipped back to Scotland. Her daughter was left behind in France.

Lady Fleming had never adapted herself to the French, and so had kept Scotland alive for Mary with her ways and her language. With her departure, and the appointment of a French governess, only faint traces of Mary's Scottish background remained. Once in a while, Mary Stuart would dress in a Scottish costume of animal skins. Her graceful and regal bearing made such a spectacle bearable to the sophisticated French court. Even if the feel and smell of the skins evoked a deep nostalgia from her buried childhood memories, over time Mary became more and more French in every way.

Her public appearances were rare. Only for festivals and on special occasions did her future subjects catch a glimpse of her. Once when carrying a torch and walking along in a religious procession, her beauty so entranced the spectators that one exclaimed, "Are you not an angel?"

Her uncle, the cardinal of Lorraine, was extremely influential in the development of her statesmanship, as well as all areas of her upbringing. But it was obvious that—as if she were born to rule and not just forced to by birth—Mary listened to her own inner guidance, as well as her family's. At twelve, the young queen revealed her sentiments on ruling, quoting Plutarch whom she felt was a philosopher worthy of a prince: "He who counterfeits a Prince's coin is punished; how much more severely should he be punished who corrupts a prince's mind, for as Plutarch tells us, 'The people of the state are apt to take after their Princes.'"

To her friend, Princess Elizabeth, she wrote:

The true grandeur of a Prince, my dear sister, is not in splendour, nor in gold or fine purple, or rich gowns and other pomps, but in prudence and wisdom: and just as a Prince is different from his subjects in his dress and manner of living, so should he differ from them in their foolish and vulgar ideas.

On another occasion she wrote: "The Prince ought not to boast principally of the parents, but should seek first of all to imitate their virtues. That is the first thing; the second is that a Prince should be well taught in arts and sciences; and, third and least is the painted blazonry of his ancestors."

When, one day Princess Claude had been naughty, insisting on drinking excessively just before going to bed, Elizabeth, the older sister, was asked to reprove her for it. Elizabeth frankly said that she too wanted water and couldn't reprove her sister. Mary responded, "We should be examples to the people. How can we reprove others unless we ourselves are faultless? A good Prince must live in such sort that great and small may take example by his virtues."

By the time Mary turned eleven, the royal nursery had become too crowded, and she was given a household of her own. Money for it had to be wrenched from the Scots. The Four Maries were allowed to join her again, and among her attendants was her physician Bourgoing, who would remain with her throughout her whole life. A band of Scottish musicians were also part of the household. Those in charge of setting up the household were warned to avoid anything superfluous or mean, "for meanness is the thing which of all others she hates." "Be assured," they were warned, "her spirit is so high that she lets her annoyance be very plainly visible, if she be unworthily treated."

A shadow in her character was being created by the blazing light of praise in which she basked day and night. It was becoming apparent that so much praise made her afraid and unable to handle criticism, for fear she was losing everyone's love. Trouble began brewing with her new governess and the running of her household. Mary's observation that Mme. de Parois was undermining her relationships was most likely accurate, but somehow Mary did not have faith that others would see that. She became nearly hysterical when she felt the troublemaking woman might turn her mother against her, becoming physically ill over the prospect. Collapse in times of stress developed into a lifelong trait, inherited from her father. Her weakness was her stomach.

Her faults were minor ones, and only magnified by the fact that Mary Stuart was to one day rule her country, and could not afford to be so sensitive. At the same time, Mary was also known to possess tremendous courage, which must have been apparent from her strength of character and buoyant spirit, but also from her great love of adventure and risk taking and her obvious athletic ability. Riding, the hunt and all outdoor activities would always give her great pleasure. Without outdoor exercise, she felt she might perish. Surprisingly, given all the extraordinary praise she received for her beguiling and feminine beauty, she often lamented she wished she had been born a man. One of her uncles, Duc de Guise, a general and a great hero in France for reclaiming Calais from the English, felt his niece's courage matched his own.

Just before her ceremony of betrothal, April 19, 1558, in the Great Hall of the newly built Louvre in Paris, the poet Bantome wrote of Mary Stuart, "Her great beauty and virtue grew in such sort that when she was about fifteen years old, her loveliness began to shine in its bright noonday, and to shame the sun itself with its brilliance, so beautiful was she."

What led this young woman, so steeped in virtues, to one day be accused of being an accomplice to the murder of her husband, and then turn around and marry his assassin, risking everything for him?

6

Queen of France

I see blood around her fair head.
—*Nostradamus*

EARLY IN THE MORNING of the second Sunday after Easter, the twenty-fourth of April 1558, masses of spectators lined the streets and paths along the procession route to the Cathedral of Notre Dame. All of Paris came to witness the wedding of their dauphin to the beautiful queen of Scots. For the first time in two hundred years, a dauphin of France was to be married in Paris. The wedding promised to be a marvel of Renaissance splendor. Henry II would spare nothing in his desire to impress upon the people and the nobles the prestige and vitality of the monarchy. It was also a great show for the Guises and the Catholics. Mary had been their puppet; they had reared her from infancy to shine on this day.

The political agreement that cemented the marriage was an example of how she was used. The secret marriage contract gave over the kingdom of Scotland, as well as her rights to the kingdom of England, unconditionally to the crown of France in the event of her death "without heirs begotten of her body." Although many would say that Mary's complicity in the secret marriage contract was the first indication that she lacked the strength of leadership and foresight necessary for a great ruler, and was instead only forever a pawn, vulnerable to those with greater powers of persuasion, she was just fifteen years old. Though by nature courageous, she had never had to develop the instincts of a street fighter like her English cousin, Elizabeth. Though she did not initiate this treachery against her country, she could have known better than to sign such an agreement. But that she did not know the implications is forgivable, given her age and experience. However, her signature, which put Scotland under domination of the French, was the seed of her tragedy.

Since childhood, Mary had remained extraordinarily loyal, not just to her Guise family, but also in her love for her very unappealing betrothed. Surrounded by the beautiful people of the court, it would seem that Mary had the chance to meet and even develop a crush or two on some of the most handsome, intelligent and charming of the young men, if only just as a facet of growing up. Her own personal attraction was boundless. Her rich and vivid humanity was irresistible to men, and she possessed an "enchantment whereby men were bewitched." But her loyalties and her innocent and pure love remained with Francois through the years, despite the fact that his nature had grown increasingly sullen and unappealing.

Francois was exceptionally weak-willed, so completely opposite from Mary's famous and brilliant uncles and the dynamic Guise clan, and Mary herself. Fourteen years old on his wedding day, it appeared Francois had not even begun to reach puberty. Like Mary, he was well aware of his princely station, but in him it developed into an unattractive self-importance, rather than a great sense of responsibility, as with Mary. The only two people in his world that he appeared to love or even care about were his mother, Catherine de' Medici, and his bride-to-be, to whom he had become an abject slave. Perhaps the eclipse at his birth portended Mary. The great numbers of people lining the streets were not waiting to see him.

Mary Stuart was one of the "rare women who in whatever station she is born, rules her world as if the talisman of which hearts are won, had been given her by a fairy Godmother."[1] Many thought she already ruled the king and queen in many ways. On her wedding day, Mary Stuart, now just fifteen, was considered the most beautiful woman in all Europe. Nearly six feet tall in an age when five feet

Mary Queen of Scots. (Giraudon/Art Resource, NY)

Decourt, Jean. Portrait of Mary (1542-1567) or perhaps a princess of the house of Habsburg. (Elisabeth of Austria, 1554-1592, Queen of France). (Giraudon/Art Resource, NY)

Above: Anonymous. Mary,
Queen of Scots.
(Victoria & Albert Museum,
London/Art Resource, NY)

Above left: Monogram of Mary Stuart
crowned, with thistles, in octogon.
Mary's cipher and motto: Sa Vertu
Martire. 16th c. embroidery.
(Victoria & Albert Museum,
London/Art Resource, NY)

Left: Somer, Paul van, I. King
James I of England.
(Art Resource, NY)

Portrait of Mary, c. 1578, possibly by Rowland Lockey.
(National Trust/Art Resource, NY)

Zuccaro, Federico. (1540-1609). Portrait of Elizabeth I of England.
(Scala/Art Resource, NY)

was average for women, and men over six feet were considered giants, she was seen as a marvel of nature. "Though tall, she was finely modeled and her beauty was of the delicate elusive sort which perplexes the artist." By all accounts, she was a breathtaking bride.

In a letter to her mother written the morning of her wedding day, Mary was over the moon with joy and gratitude for all her blessings, and thrilled to be finally marrying Francois. She found it nearly impossible to express her feelings. The display of wealth and pageantry of the royal wedding was so lavish, so magnificent and so sumptuous, that chroniclers, like Mary, also found it almost impossible to find the words to describe the spectacle.

Mary Stuart must have appeared to be a goddess; hardly an earthly creature, more like the queen of some enchanted fairy kingdom. Defying tradition, Mary may have been the first bride in France to ever wear white on her wedding day. White had been always before the color of mourning for French queens. But white was the color that most suited Mary and set off her exquisite coloring, her milky white and perfect complexion, her now lush auburn hair and dreamy chestnut eyes. Her gown was so sumptuous, so rich, that a pen fell from the hands of one contemporary writer as he contemplated the impossibility of adequately describing its magnificence. It seems everyone was having a hard time writing that day. The gown itself was of white and silver cloth, and glittered with sparkling precious stones. Two young girls carried the extremely long train. Her cape was of violet velvet embroidered with gold. On her head, she wore a golden crown with pearls, diamonds, rubies, sapphires and emeralds. In the center was a carbuncle valued at the time at 500,000 crowns.

Throughout the procession to the cathedral, during the Mass, and as the wedding party made its way to the bishop's palace for the lavish banquet afterward, heralds flung gold and silver coins into the crowd, shouting, "Largesse! Largesse!" to excite and impress the crowds even further.

At some point during the banquet and ball that lasted until four in the afternoon, the crown grew too heavy for the new queen-dauphiness' long and slender neck to support, and Henry ordered a lord-in-waiting to stand behind her and hold the crown over her head. The entire court then traveled, men by horseback and women by litter, to the palace of the Parliament for the evening's ball and entertainment. Vast numbers of people lined the way to watch the royals pass by. Their new queen-dauphiness rode in a golden litter with her new mother-in-law the queen. Her bridegroom and his gentlemen rode behind on horses draped in crimson velvet trappings.

When the evening's entertainment resumed at the palace on St. Christophe's Street, so many candles were lit it looked like broad daylight, and everyone and everything glittered like the heavens. Wearing a frosted cloth of gold and gems, the duke of Guise acted as master of ceremonies. Much of the evening's elaborate entertainment had an esoteric flavor to it, in keeping with the Guise family's true affiliation with such thought, and seems, if not to rival a Las Vegas show of today or the half time at the Super Bowl, to at least be a harbinger.

The entertainment began with a procession of seven planets. Mercury was dressed in white satin with a gold girdle; Mars was in armor and Venus in floating draperies. Artificial gold and silver horses then passed by the royal table, followed by nine muses who arrived by chariots drawn by two white horses.

The triumphant finale was a brilliant pageant of ships, with six vessels covered with cloths of gold and crimson velvet, their sails with silver linen. The ships were ingeniously propelled along the floor of the ballroom. Appearing to be tossed about by a stormy sea, they pitched and rolled. In each ship was a masked prince dressed in gold cloth. As each vessel passed the royal table, a prince invited one of the ladies to sit beside him on his ship's throne. There was a ship each for Mary, Catherine de' Medici, the queen of Navarre, and Princesses Elizabeth, Claude and Marguerite, the daughters of Henry II. As each ship embarked with its new passenger, the seas grew calm to symbolize the happy future ahead for the bride and groom, and it was hopeful, too, the kingdom.

The seas would remain calm for Mary only a few months longer. Her blessed life was about to have a monumental turn of fortune and head toward far more dangerous waters.

PARIS CELEBRATED THE ROYAL marriage with fifteen days of festivals and fetes. Given that it did not appear that Francois had reached puberty, it is questionable whether the marriage was ever truly consummated in the biblical sense, at least in the beginning. Rumors abounded that the king's "withered anatomy" prevented any hopes of an heir.

Pressure on Mary must have been enormous to produce the longed-for Guise-Valois heir and ensure the Guise family a long line of succession for the French throne. Several times, she became ill, and word spread she was with child. Mary may have even convinced herself this was so for a while, knowing what conceiving a child would mean. Some have suggested that she may have been naive enough about such matters not to realize the extent of her husband's undeveloped sexuality. This speculation could have some merit if she were reared in the puritanical Scottish court, but it is obvious she was not under glass at the French court.

Despite the lack of marital passion, for one with such a loving and passionate nature, no breath of scandal ever touched Mary's name throughout their brief married life. "On the contrary, her reasonableness, her prudence, her thoughtfulness, her devoted attention to her husband supplied a theme for many pens." To be a "brilliant, vigorous girl, unequally mated, prominent in a jealous, merciless society, and come out unscathed" was miraculous.

During her years in France, Mary made only one enemy, but it was the most formidable enemy: Catherine de' Medici. Mary soon discovered that her marriage severely restricted her freedom. Just as the Queen Mother monitored every breath her children took, she now spied on Mary, noting every movement, word and look of her daughter-in-law. Growing up, Mary had done much the same with the Queen Mother—spending most afternoons in Queen Catherine's presence chamber, studying her every move as she prepared herself for her future role. Mary had preferred this to being with companions, even though Catherine, despite being impressed by Mary's beauty, precocity and devotion to her son, was not overly fond of her. For a long time, the two seemed inseparable. Finally her high and noble spirit outgrew the tutorship, and Mary declared:

"The daughter of a Florentine trader is not the equal of the heir of a hundred kings." Catherine never forgave her.

Francois gave his wife no sympathy or intellectual companionship. This Mary received from her continued studies and from the intellectuals of the court. Husband and wife did however both love to be enormously active, always dancing, riding, hawking or hunting, despite the fact that both were often too ill to participate. Mary adapted to her husband and he was as devoted as he was capable of being. In her marriage, she lived in a "position of splendid constraint." Mary had become thoroughly French and loved the life of the court.

The first critical turn of fate, which seemed to set off a sudden chain of catastrophes for Mary, was the death, on November 17, 1558, of Mary Tudor, first child of Henry VIII, who had become queen of England after her brother Edward's early demise. Physicians of the time proclaimed her death was caused by dropsy, or an excessive accumulation of dangerous fluid in the tissue also known as edema. Now it is clear her symptoms indicated she died of ovarian cancer.

A zealous Catholic, Mary Tudor had returned England to the pope and allied her country with Catholic Spain by marrying King Philip, and she was greatly hated. As part of her own tyrannical reformation, she persecuted and burned to death countless Protestants and threw countless more into prison. Her holocaust was blamed for the crops being stunted and for the severely cold weather that summer. The day she died, all of England, except the Catholics, rejoiced.

Perpetually panicked over the prospect of never producing an heir, Mary Tudor remained childless despite trying every remedy possible. Even though to the Protestants, Mary Tudor was legally illegitimate—since her father had annulled his marriage with her mother, Catherine of Aragon—in the eyes of the Catholic Church and the Catholics of England, she was the only legitimate heir. Her half sister Elizabeth, unmarried and twenty-five, was next in line to the throne according to the Protestants. But as Henry VIII's marriage to Elizabeth's mother Anne Bolyn was never recognized by the Catholic Church, Elizabeth was considered by the Church to be illegitimate and not in any way in line to succeed.

In line of succession after Elizabeth was Mary Stuart, by the fact that all three of them shared the same grandfather, Henry VII. However, Henry VIII had passed a law disallowing any foreigner to wear the crown of England, which meant Mary for one. Nevertheless, "By the laws of primogeniture, Mary Stuart had an excellent claim to the English crown."

As if by promulgating it, it was so, whether or not the English Parliament or the people agreed, and with no military backing behind the claim, the French king proclaimed Mary Stuart queen of England, Ireland, and Wales, as well as queen of Scotland and queen-dauphinesse of France, and her husband, his son, king. Whether she agreed to it or not, and there is a chance but no proof that she did not, Mary and Francois added England, Ireland and Wales to their coat of arms. It can be certain that her Guise uncles unquestionably supported the French king. Their power base would be enormous. Philip II of Spain and Henry II of France had been settling their differences and were poised, using Mary Stuart as their pawn, to "dismember England between them at their leisure. All over Europe, bets were being laid that the new queen of England would not keep her rickety throne for six months."[2]

For the rest of her life Mary would be haunted by her father-in-law's and her uncles' audacity. Any action Mary would take in the future was seen by Elizabeth through the filter of Mary's legitimate and imminent threat to Elizabeth's shaky claims to the throne. Born a princess, then branded and treated like a bastard and her mother beheaded before the age of three, Elizabeth learned early how to survive. But not until Mary finally placed her beautiful swan-like neck on the executioner's block could Elizabeth feel secure that the throne was hers. Mary's destiny with the executioner was sealed by the arrogance of the men who loved her.

A tribute to her boldness and determination in the face of such powerful enemies, Elizabeth's coronation was a triumph, both for her and her mother. By claiming the crown, she was able to erase her own stigma of illegitimacy and her mother's reputation as a whore. The country loved her completely. At twenty-five she was perfect—a fresh and beautiful face after the sour and nasty Mary Tudor—and she was Protestant. It seemed she was born to the throne. Throughout her reign, "the one thing that [could] be said of her with absolute certainty is that she loved England and England's people with a deep, abiding, selfless love." She was wedded to the people. After witnessing the power a man could have over a woman, as her own father epitomized, there was no way that Elizabeth I would ever give her soul or spirit away to any man.

Elizabeth was the Virgin Queen, detached from bodily desires in an archetypical sense, although hardly a virgin in the real sense. Her people did not seem to question this disparity. The word "virgin," though, had actually taken on new meaning over time: In ancient matriarchal societies, a virgin was a woman on her own, not married and most likely a temple priestess, initiated in the art of using the energy of the goddess to heal. As the tide turned, men began to control women's bodies to gain power and wealth away from matrilineal lines and these powerful priestesses. Even if this knowledge has been forgotten at the conscious level, it remains in the collective unconscious as a distant, primordial memory called an archetype. Carmen Poulter, in her book *Angels and Archetypes*, describes archetypes as being by their very nature alive. "They are connected to our instincts and trigger us emotionally. They provide a psychological map that can help us identify our stage of growth and our place in the world. They bring forward the parts of ourselves that have been unconscious. When an archetype constellates, a psychological field radiates from the deep unconscious."[3]

As the Virgin Queen, Elizabeth was the pure mother, offering herself up as mother to all without sexual guilt, reflecting the upswelling of the Protestant Reformation, and the Catholic faith, whose Virgin gave birth without sex. This new mother of England, Elizabeth I, offered herself to the people without complication or corruption. On the other hand, Mary Stuart had saintly status in France. Yet, in only a few years, she would be called a whore and murderess in her own country of Scotland. Still, it was Mary who became queen of a people, the "Queen of Scots," whereas it was always simply "Elizabeth I of England."

SOON AFTER ELIZABETH'S ascension, the first of a string of tragedies propelled Mary Stuart along toward her true destiny, as prophesied. The famous astrologer of the French court, Nostradamus, first published his prophesies in 1555 in his celebrated work called *The Centuries*. Though written in ambiguous quatrains, and covering all the centuries through to the new millennium four hundred and fifty years away, even today many can read into them events in recent history. One quatrain hung like a black cloud over the crowd gathered on June 30, 1559, for one of the series of tournaments being held to celebrate the marriages of Henry's fourteen-year-old daughter Elizabeth to the recent widower of Mary Tudor, Philip II of Spain, and his sister Marguerite to the duke of Savoy. The court could talk of nothing else but what to wear to all the festivities in honor of the two magnificent weddings. Mary was very much involved in the planning.

Foreign soldiers, princes of the blood and the noble men and ladies of the court all glittered in raiment and turned their attention to the final contest of the tournament. As the king took the field looking gallant and handsome, wearing black and white, the favorite colors of his mistress Diane de Poitiers, all felt more than a little concern for their monarch as the words of Nostradamus tempered the crowd.

> The young lion will master the old
> On the martial field by a single combat;
> In a golden [cage] his eyes will be burst open,
> Two divisions in one, then a cruel death.

Mounting his big, bay war-horse Le Malheureux, the king entered the lists, in high humor. His love of jousting bordered on madness. The king broke three lances with the duke of Savoy, the duke of Guise and Jacques de Lorge, count of Montgomery, a Norman of Scottish blood, who was colonel of the archers of the Scots Guard and a man of renowned courage. Since no one had been unseated, the king felt unsatisfied and challenged Montgomery to break one last lance with him. Montgomery refused. Though the light was fading, the king's consummate passion to excel commanded Montgomery to continue.

Seven years before, another court astrologer, Luc Gauric, had predicted Henry's death in a duel, a prediction no one ever took seriously, because the king never involved himself in single combat. Now everyone held their breath—especially Catherine, who sent a messenger down to the field asking him to quit for the day. The queen had had two visions of ill omens about the tournament. (In her daughter Marguerite's diaries, she tells of a dream her mother had the night before, describing Henry's death just as it was about to happen.) Henry insisted on one more joust in Catherine's honor.

One pass was unsatisfactory. Henry commanded a second. This time the lances splintered. For some reason, Montgomery neglected to throw away the broken lance and it jammed the king's helmet, as he speeded past on his horse. The jagged shaft burst open the king's visor and a fragment of wood penetrated and broke into the king's forehead above the right eye. Another splinter pierced his throat. The king was knocked unconscious.

Henry was carried off to the Hotel des Tournelles, where he lay unconscious for nine days. The physicians felt helpless in their efforts to revive him. "Half a dozen criminals were promptly decapitated, and subjected to similar wounds, which physicians hastened to examine in an attempt to find the best method of treatment."[4] On the eighth of July, in a brief lucid moment, he ordered the wedding of Marguerite and the duke of Savoy to proceed immediately. The wedding was performed amid a flood of tears. Mary and Francois did not attend, but stayed close by the king's bedside.

On July 9, as Henry felt himself dying, he called for Francois and began, "My son, I recommend to you the Church and my people." He found it impossible to speak further. Offering the dauphin his blessing, he kissed him. Spent, Henri could not go on. The virulent infection had swollen his hands and feet to gross proportions. His breathing was very painful and that evening he grew paralyzed. He died at one in the morning of July 10.

Though many were suspicious, Montgomery was never officially blamed. Some—those who knew of the Scots Guard affilia-

tion with the houses of Guise and Lorraine—while they were out-
wardly guards for the Valois—suspected that Nostradamus's quatrain was a code, a signal and part of an elaborately contrived plan.
The death of Henry was of enormous benefit to the Guise and Lorraine families. For the next decade, the houses of Valois and Guise-
Lorraine would conspire and battle for the throne of France.
Charismatic, dynamic but ruthless young men of two generations
from both families would be lost in the effort.

But for now, and only for a brief time, the Guise-Lorraine family controlled all of France. Fulfilling their highest hopes and
dreams, their young niece, not yet sixteen years old, ascended the
throne of France, now queen of two countries, with claims to a third.

Soon after the death of the king, Mary wrote to her mother
about the widowed queen: "She is much troubled still, and I fear she
will fall seriously sick with grief; I believe that were it not that the
king her son is so obedient that he will do nothing but what she
wishes, she would soon die, which would be the greatest misfortune
that could befall this poor country and all of us."

The room was draped completely in black, curtains were drawn
and only two candles lit when the Spanish ambassadors entered to
pay their respects to Queen Catherine, herself dressed from head to
toe in black, except for a collar of ermine. She could barely speak.
Sitting with her, the beautiful Mary was a counterpoint in all white.
It had been only fifteen months since her wedding. She gave a
pretty speech and sang the praises of her uncles, as they would have
wished her to do.

7

Queen Dowager

LA CORBIE: Knox has torn the Mother of God from oot the sky o' Scotland
And has trampit her celestial blue goon amang the muck and mire
and has blotted oot every name by which ye praise her—
Stella Maris, Star of the Sea, Holy Mother, Notre Dame,
Oor Lady o' Perpetual Succour.
MARY: But if he has torn her frae the blue sky what has he left in her place?
LA CORBIE: A black hole, a jaggit gash, Naithin'.

—*Liz Lochead*

BESIEGED BY FOES, holed up in Edinburgh Castle with only three thousand Frenchmen to defend her, the courageous Marie de Guise was now a forlorn and tragic figure.

On the eleventh of August 1559, the Scottish Parliament went completely around the monarchy, Marie de Guise as regent and Mary and Francois, and declared a Protestant confession of faith, abolishing the pope from holding any jurisdiction in the country. Celebration of the Mass was no longer permitted. Anyone saying or hearing Mass would be punished by confiscation of goods for the first offense, banishment for the second and death for the third. This act was not only historic in initiating the Protestant Reformation, and aligning Scotland with Protestant England rather than Catholic France, it also forever from then on undermined the power of the monarchy in Scotland. The requirement to have the assent of the queen on such an enactment was completely ignored.

The implications of such an act were not yet visible. Thus, Mary would remain unaware of the extent of the peril lying ahead for her when she returned to rule her native land. Aligning with the Protestant Scots had little to do with religious zealotry on Elizabeth's part, and everything to do with checkmating Catholic Mary Stuart, should she ever try to return to Scotland to reign as queen.

As a counter move, before his death, Henry II, under the guidance of the Guise's and the papacy, was determined, despite the financial exhaustion of his own country, to send a large force of troops to Scotland to protect the throne for Mary and Francois. His intention was to "overcome the heretics and schematics, and force the power into Scottish Catholic hands, to chastise and punish their great temerity and arrogance, for the honour of the Creator, the exaltation of His Holy Name, and the increase of our holy faith and religion."[1]

Henry's move would only serve to inflame the Protestants, rendering any further diplomacy on the part of Marie de Guise fruitless. Knowing the danger her mother was in, Mary wrote to reassure her that, "Francois has so much care to aid you that you will be content with him, for he has thus promised me, and I will not let him forget it, nor the Queen Mother either who has honored us by weeping copiously upon hearing of your troubles. I have urged her so that I am sure she will not fail to send you all the help that she can."

Health failing, Marie de Guise fought resolutely against overwhelming odds. But the constitutional resistance deposed her from her regency. Afraid her mother would remain prisoner and fearing the loss of her own kingdom, the sixteen-year-old Mary shed "bitter tears incessantly and at length from anguish and sorrow took to her bed." She turned to her uncle, the cardinal of Lorraine, now called by many the "Pope and King of France," and reproached him for putting her Scottish realm in such peril by his policies.

Ascension to the throne by frail and melancholy Francois II, after the death of his father King Henry II, initiated a critical period in French history. Francois was "eager and ambitious, and stirred to vivacity by the spirit of his wife," yet he was also "weak and submissive." For the most part, Mary was "keenly alive and responsive to the far-reaching policy of her uncles, and like them, determined to do her part with a masterful hand." Thus dominated, Francois turned over the governing of his kingdom to his wife's uncles of the House of Guise.

Rising to political supremacy, the cardinal of Lorraine, his brother the duke and friends had summoned a council and urged all means be taken to crush the Protestants in Scotland. Mary's half brother James and other lords were to be assassinated, but Elizabeth I's ambassador, Throckmorton, warned them in time. Throckmorton had written his sovereign, "Seeing how the House of Guise ruleth, with whom I am in very small grace and that the Queen of Scotland, who is a great doer here and taketh all upon her, hath so small an opinion of me, I shall be able to do small service with her."

Her brothers thwarted Marie de Guise's instincts, "to deal in Scotland in a spirit of conciliation, introducing much gentleness and moderation into the administration of justice." That said, Marie did have the strength to oppose her brothers when she strongly disagreed, even if they thought she would undo everything with her tender methods.

Her assessment that the Scottish government could use her help was well founded. Laws were for the most part as uncivilized as the people. But her able, skillful and gallant efforts were unappreciated. As Knox would say with acid contempt and quite unfairly, "A crown was put upon her head . . . as seemly a sight . . . as to put a saddle upon the back of a cow."

Mary begged her mother to trust that God would see her through her adversities, as He somehow always had. Nevertheless, horribly swollen and in great pain from dropsy, Marie of Guise died near midnight on June 10, 1560. Knox saw in her terrible end God's vengeance on her. On her deathbed, Marie met with her stepson, James, and a few of the nobles, to tell them her brothers' policies were based on fatal ambition. She admitted she was often forced to follow an unwise policy, and begged them not to let this jeopardize her daughter's claims to the crown.

Although the news of her death reached France on the eighteenth of June, her daughter was not told for another ten days. Mary received the news with wrenching grief and collapsed in her bed, physically undone by her enormous sorrow. Despite the fact that she had spent only a total of seven years with her mother, and had not actually seen her for over eight, Mary was an extraordinarily devoted daughter. "Mary loved her mother dearly. Indeed, her affections were intense wherever they were placed."

THE SUPREMACY OF THE Guise's had only six more months to go. Mary's brief reign as queen of France was about to end. Without an heir, the Guise power base rested solely on the weak shoulders of the sickly Francois. People had begun to turn in horror of the king. His breath was fetid and his face was covered with alarming red blotches, creating rumors that he actually suffered from leprosy. His enemies spread the rumor that the king's only cure was taking baths in the blood of freshly killed infants and young children. Peasants hid their children as he passed. Francois was heartbroken to see the defection of his people. "He grew more feeble and more unhappy as the evil consequences of the Guise policy became increasingly apparent to him."

On the frosty late afternoon of November 16, 1560, the eve of a month-long hunting expedition, Francois returned from a day's hunt with a fierce earache. He fainted the next day during vespers in the chapel of the Jacobins. Plagued by an ear infection from childhood, his facial deformity was most likely eczema, a by-product of his constant respiratory infection. A fever had developed from a severe abscess in his right ear that surgery of the day could not cure. Mary never left his bedside.

In the beginning, the Guises were desperate to conceal the seriousness of the king's situation. Rumors accusing opposing religious and political factions of being the cause of the king's undoing flew all around the court. It was even suggested that Catherine de' Medici so disliked her daughter-in-law that she poisoned her son in order to deprive Mary of the throne, which was as unlikely as any of the other rumors. However, the truth was, "upon the ebbing days of the youthful monarch there depended the lives and liberties of thousands, perhaps the fate of the religious freedoms of the world."[2]

Trying all available remedies of the day, the king was subjected to purgations and bleedings, and a massive dose of rhubarb, which actually brought him some relief. But then the horrible headaches and illness intensified. Masses and prayers were said. Processions were ordered. The Guises, watching their fortunes ebb with the king's life force, raged at all the doctors. Mary and Catherine never left the patient's side. By December 3, inflammation had spread to the king's brain and there was nothing to save him. On December 5, a month short of his seventeenth birthday, Francois II breathed his last breath after a disastrous reign of sixteen months. No one wept for him but his mother and his young widow, who was three days away from her eighteenth birthday.

Knox's poison pen had a heyday. "Lo! The potent hand of God sends unto us a wonderful and most joyful deliverance, for unhappy Francis suddenly perisheth of a rotten ear, that deaf ear that would never hear the word of God."

The French Huguenots, finally rid of the Guises and therefore the papacy, were exultant. Calvin, echoing Knox's sentiments, wrote, "Did you ever hear of anything more timely than the death of the little king? There was no remedy for the worst evils when God suddenly revealed Himself from Heaven, and He who pierced the father's eye, struck off the ear of the son."

Personal rivalries, plots and counterplots, fanned by religious fanaticism and economic discontent of the masses, seriously imperiled the monarchy. France was on the eve of civil war. It was a troubled heritage Francois and Mary left to a neurotic little boy of eleven, Francois' younger brother, now King Charles IX.

With Francois' death, Mary was suddenly left bereft of any solid support. Instead of queen of France, she was now queen dowager. Her uncles no longer wielded any real power. Her mother was dead, and the Scottish throne she had given her life to protect for her daughter appeared to have no real meaning for the Scots. Power was in the hands of the Parliament. No longer able to offer the support of the French to her country, Mary seemed to have little value to the Scots. On top of everything, her childhood friends, Elizabeth, Claude and now Francois were all gone.

Worn out from caring for her husband in his last days, and still grieving the loss of her mother, Mary had little reserves to strengthen her against the overpowering grief she felt at the loss of her beloved companion of twelve years. Their bond had been forged from before they met, and cemented the first day they set eyes on each other when she was five and he was four. Rarely were they ever apart. And for nearly three years, they shared the intimacy of husband and wife. Mary was not grieving for her fortunes. She was grieving for Francois. Most likely, she did not give a thought to her future or her predicament for many, many days.

To give herself fully over to her grief, Mary, wearing white again, shut herself up in a black room lit only by torches. One of the poems she wrote during this time expresses her touching sorrow:

Wherever I may be
In the woods or in the fields
Whatever the hour of the day
Be it dawn or the eventide
My heart still feels it yet
The eternal regret . . .
As I sink into my sleep
The absent one is near
Alone upon my couch
I feel his beloved touch
In work or in repose
We are forever close . . .

The Venetian ambassador, who seemed to always feel a special tenderness toward Mary, observed: "Soon the death of the late King will be forgotten by all except his little wife, who has been widowed, has lost France, and has little hope of Scotland . . . her unhappiness and incessant tears call forth general compassion."

MARY EMERGED FROM her forty days and forty nights of formal mourning her own woman. Even before her husband's last breath, speculation about her next husband was rampant. The list of eligible bachelors was long. Each prospective bridegroom represented a different future for the young widow, and widely varying political scenarios for the men and countries involved. There were prospects should she try to gain the throne of England, prospects should she try to return to Scotland as queen. Both of those avenues appeared to require an army as well. She could again become queen of France by marrying her brother-in-law, the young king of France, who was quite fond of her, but there, odds were slim she could wrench power back from Catherine de' Medici, now queen regent.

Despite all the advice, Mary was going to decide her own fate this time, and everyone was impressed with her strength.

Throckmorton, Elizabeth's ambassador to the French court, was taken aback by the change in her. Where he felt little regarded while Mary was in subjugation to her husband and her uncles, he felt he was finally able to get to know her now that she was on her own. Now one of her biggest fans, he wrote back to Elizabeth, who was extremely interested in any tidbit about her cousin, that Mary showed "both a great wisdom for her years, modesty, and also of great judgment in the wise handling of herself and her matters, which, increasing with her years, cannot but turn greatly to her commendation, reputation, honour and great benefit of her and her country. And for my part," Throckmorton's letter continued, "I see her behaviour to be such, and her wisdom and kingly modesty so great, in that she thinketh herself not too wise, but is content to be ruled by good counsel and wise men (which is a great virtue in a Prince or Princess), and which argueth a great judgment and wisdom in her."

With his genuine praise of Mary's great sense of responsibility and obvious maturity, Throckmorton was also trying to make a point with Elizabeth, known for her coarse wit, whose own court was described as entirely frivolous. Of Elizabeth's court, Throckmorton said, "Nothing is treated earnestly, and though all things go wrong they jest, and he who invents the most ways of wasting time is regarded as one worthy of honour."

Remarkably, the Protestants, so judgmental of Mary, never

maligned Elizabeth for her outrageous behavior. Her advisor, Sir William Cecil, believed Elizabeth "wished to do as her father did." She did follow in her father's footsteps, provoking gossip and scandal, and advancing her personal desires at the expense of her reputation. Just like her father, the Virgin Queen achieved "sovereign mastery of her sexual life, at the expense of others." And like her father, her lovers were worse off from their encounter, while she remained unscathed. Of high intelligence, possessing a high and courageous spirit and toughened by adversity, Elizabeth never considered herself to be illegitimate. "Truculent, violent, disagreeable, arrogant, always majestic: such was the Queen of Hampton Court. Her loud authoritative voice echoed fearsomely down the long galleries of the great palace, and the hive of mighty and lowly subjects who served her there, however they plotted and cursed her for the stubborn woman that she was, trembled at the sound."[3] Cecil always took every precaution against the possibility of Elizabeth's assassination, especially by poison. Her treatment of her ministers and attendants was capricious and despotic. She could be approachable and amiable one moment, peevish and ill humored the next. Her words could cut as cruelly as swords. Anything, even playing cards, could be the cause of her titanic fury. Her words often carried the threat of violence.

As strong as she appeared, Elizabeth had radical weaknesses. In every emergency she was irresolute, implementing inconsistent policies, and erratic conduct. "The greatest crimes to stain her character were committed under the influence of terror."[4] To the end of her life, she was haunted by imaginary fears, which impaired her will and her mind over time. Elizabeth seemed able all her life to deflect the judgment of others as of no concern, where Mary absorbed it. Elizabeth's subjects always saw her as a great and magnanimous sovereign, the idol of her people and the terror of her enemies.

Just months before, on September 8, in a strange foretelling of the major and stunning turning point in Mary's life, Amy Dudley, wife of Robert Dudley, Elizabeth's lover, horse master and childhood friend, was found dead at the bottom of a flight of stone steps, her neck broken. Elizabeth's reaction was flippant. She had been openly and scandalously carrying on with Dudley, who was by far the handsomest man at the court. Under his tutelage, she had become a huntress and a horsewoman. But why would she not casually have her lover's wife murdered? How many times had she seen her father do it? Although she appeared to transcend the disgrace, Cecil advised Elizabeth that if she married Dudley, the "ruin of the realm was sure to follow." Where Mary lost everything for her, perhaps pardonable, indiscretion, Elizabeth carried on brazenly through hers.

ENCLOSED IN A LEADEN VASE, Francois' heart now rested on a pillar within the cathedral of Saint-Denis, the traditional resting place of French kings. Part of a bittersweet poem written during this time reveals that, though Mary was rising to what was expected of her, her own heart was still heavy with grief.

> In my sad and
> gentle song
> Of profound
> lamentation
> I look deeply
> At incomparable
> loss,
> And in burning
> sighs
> Pass my best
> years.

Having faced her "incomparable" grief, Mary transcended her childhood and found great strength for one so young, strength that gave her, at nineteen, the ability to travel to the homes of friends and relatives gathering opinions and advice, and then with certainty choose for herself the direction her life would take. Before she would have been led by others.

Acting on her first instincts, Mary wrote the Scottish Estates a

Carol Schaefer

gentle-toned letter, informing them of Francois' death and that she wished to return to Scotland as their queen, and hoped this would be most agreeable with her subjects.

At the same time, there was a prospective groom being dangled who appeared to offer a continuation of the grand life and prestige that was by now so much a part of who she thought she was. Besides, she could not look for love yet, and probably could not even imagine it. So her decisions were made, not with a romantic but with a practical heart and mind. This other possibility, living in the grandeur of the Spanish court, included a prospective groom who was nearly a replica of Francois. Don Carlos, son of Philip of Spain, was small and slightly deformed physically, an epileptic and had a noticeable speech impediment. What he would never have was the child's heart to love him despite everything as Francois did with Mary. Mary's happiness would have to be found in the trappings of royalty and with the fact she would be close to her childhood friend again. Elizabeth, Henri II's daughter, had married King Philip of Spain, Don Carlos' father. And he was Catholic.

Around the time negotiations were beginning for the possible betrothal, Don Carlos had a serious tumble down a long staircase while chasing a serving girl. The resultant injury to the brain, and the surgery to try to repair the paralysis it caused, left him prone to fits of homicidal mania. He also, afterward, developed a crush on his stepmother Elizabeth, and developed a hatred for his father for being married to her.

Despite the obviously miserable relationship awaiting her in Spain, Mary was accepting of her destiny, should that path open up squarely, and was praised for her maturity in setting aside any personal needs. Throckmorton wrote, again with his own queen's irresponsible behavior in the back of his mind: "As far as I can learn, she more esteemeth the continuation of her honour and to marry one that may uphold her to be great than she passeth to please her fancy by taking one that is accompanied with such small benefit or alliance, as thereby her estimation and fame is not increased."

Catherine de' Medici, having wrested the power in France for herself, was not about to let any of it go. In no way would she enable

70

the Guise brothers to get a foot back in the door, or Mary to have that much power again. Her daughter Elizabeth's position could be undermined. So Catherine offered her daughter Marguerite to Spain, and suddenly Mary was no longer so desirable. However, it took Mary a while to let go of her daydreams of the good life at the Spanish court. What else had she known? What else had she been bred for?

Meanwhile, her future husband, Lord Robert Darnley, a good-looking young man who shared some of the same royal blood of England as Mary, the husband who would be the cause of her great tragedy, came to call, prodded by his ambitious mother. She barely took note of him.

Also coming to pay respects was a contingent from Scotland, led by her half brother James. As the Scottish nobles got used to the possibility of their young queen's arrival, some began to see the advantages. For James, especially, her return could be seen to be of benefit, especially, because he assumed he would have his younger sister under his thumb. James had already won the confidence of Elizabeth I. Her ambassador, Throckmorton, described James as "one of the most virtuous noblemen, and one in whom religion, sincerity and magnanimity as much reign as ever he knew in any man in any nation."

Much of their discussion involved Mary's handling of the religious issue. As nearly everyone else, including Philip of Spain, had also advised, tolerance seemed the key to successfully win over the realm. This policy, though contrary to her uncles', was thoroughly aligned with Mary's own nature. James directly came out and asked her to embrace Protestantism, and she respectfully declined, drawing the distinction between private worship and public policy.

Mary's beliefs were clearly stated to Throckmorton: "I will be plain with you," she told him. "The religion which I profess I take to be the most acceptable to God; and, indeed, neither do I know, nor desire to know any other. Constancy becometh all folks well, and none better than Princes, and such as have rule over realms, and especially in matters of religion. I have been brought up in this religion; and who aught would credit me in anything if I should show myself higher in this case." As the legal penalty in Scotland for being caught a third time saying or hearing Mass was death, this was a courageous response. She wished nothing less than tolerance and mercy for the Protestants, and asked for nothing more for herself than to be able to privately hear Mass. But given the fanaticism of many Protestants, such statements could easily put her life in danger, should she follow through with her own private worship when reaching Scotland.

Toward the end of her travels, while visiting the court of Lorraine, Mary collapsed with another debilitating tertian fever, to which she was so prone, and was unable to journey to Rheims for her brother-in-law's coronation. Her grandmother Antoinette collected Mary and brought her to Joinville for a long convalescence, which also, as it turned out, served as an enforced retreat. While there, she made up her mind on the course of action she would take and returned to court firmly decided.

Mary was received in brilliant splendor after being three months away from the French court, just as she could expect to be treated the rest of her life should she choose to remain queen dowager of France. Her estates in France were more than adequate to maintain her in regal fashion and it was very likely an attractive prince would show up in a short while.

A luxurious, pampered, but predictable life in France where she was admired and dearly loved, or a new, unpredictable life in Scotland, with few friends, far fewer amenities and many, many enemies? For now, these were her two real choices—as if while standing on the edge of a dense green forest, she chose to forge her own path, rather than take the one already trod. It had always been in her deepest nature to take the more heroic journey. Full of the spirit of adventure throughout her life, and not the least conservative, instinctively she knew she would wither in a safe life, no matter how beckoning and reasonable.

Only those who could not give up such grandeur, or who had always longed for such opulence but never had it, would be unable to understand, and would attribute her decision to other reasons, such as ego fulfillment in having her very own kingdom. For a bright and beautiful young woman, so cosseted and with everything going for her, to choose the more daring course took amazing courage. And because she had never experienced anything but, she expected to succeed.

As she was deciding, so was Scotland. On the tenth of June, her brother Lord James wrote to her practically extending an invitation, if not the royal carpet. Sir William Maitland also wrote, offering his devoted service should she decide to come to Scotland. It was dawning on the Protestant lords that Mary's near-claim to the throne of England might be of considerable value to Scotland.

Aware of the importance of her relationship with Elizabeth I, should she choose Scotland, Mary had begun to feel out their relationship through Throckmorton for months. Always gracious when speaking of his mistress, Mary had wanted more than anything to receive a portrait of the English queen, her cousin. The portrait and the civility of the relationship were offered like a dangling carrot in exchange for Mary's signature on the Treaty of Edinburgh. The treaty had established peace between England, Scotland and France the previous summer. French troops were to be withdrawn from Scotland, and both England and France were to desist from interfering there. As this was drawn up before Francois' death, it further stipulated that Mary Stuart and Francois were to stop bearing the English coat of arms.

Mary refused to sign, saying she needed to consult with her lords when finally in Scotland. Clearly, she wanted to further negotiate succession to the English throne, rather than just throw it away for herself or her heirs, since she had such a legitimate claim to it. Since her young husband's death, she had dropped the arms of England and Ireland and the title to show her good intentions.

ENGLISH SHIPS PATROLLED the sea between France and Scotland, and so in preparation for her return to her homeland, Mary sent a messenger to Elizabeth to request a passport of safe-conduct. Elizabeth asked the messenger, d'Oysel, whether he had brought a ratified Treaty of Edinburgh with him. When he replied no and Elizabeth realized she did not get her way, she blasted him with her full fury. Word of Elizabeth's anger at having her will thwarted, of course, reached Mary. The next time Mary saw Throckmorton, she suggested with a touch of satire that perhaps they should draw apart, just in case he angered her by his comments, and she released upon him such a display of "choler and stomache," as Elizabeth had vented on her messenger, d'Oysel. "I know not how far I may with my passions be transported," Mary explained. "But I like not to have so many witnesses of my passions as your mistress has of hers."

On another occasion, Mary further revealed her opinions and her self-assurance to Throckmorton: "It will be thought very strange among all princes and countries that she should first animate my subjects against me, and now being a widow, impeach my going into my own country." Whether they understood the reasons for either woman's refusal, Mary's to sign right away or Elizabeth's to offer safe-conduct as a result, all were concerned that the much hoped-for beneficial and tender relationship of cousins was already in extreme jeopardy.

For much of her life, Mary took the symbol that her mother had also loved—a phoenix rising from the ashes—as her own. Perhaps she was unconsciously inspired to from having survived so many intense fevers, collapsing in them, but then finding renewed strength as she came out the other side. Again in July, a month before she left for Scotland, another bout of tertian fever leveled her. She came out of this one rising magnificently to Elizabeth's tauntings. Rather than being intimidated, the eighteen-year-old queen of Scots reacted with cool courage, drawing strength from her regal nature, aware that all eyes were on her. She apologized to Throckmorton for involving him in acquiring a passport that she in fact did not require. She had reached French shores safely as a young child, despite threats then, and she certainly could return home safely as a young woman now, with the help of her own people. "Obviously," Mary observed. "Elizabeth values disobedient Scots to their lawful sovereign."

Elizabeth was disagreeably surprised by the political acumen and seductive qualities of her young cousin, and expressed misgivings about the "sort of havoc the pretty creature might create

among the hot-blooded, volatile Scottish warlords." With eloquence and affection, Mary gave Throckmorton her last word on
the subject.

Monsieur l'Ambassadeur, if my preparations were not so much
advanced as they are, peradventure the Queen, your Mistress'
unkindness might stay my voyage; but now I am determined to
adventure the matter, whatsoever come of it; I trust the wind
will be so favourable as I shall not need to come on the coast of
England; and if I do, Monsieur l'Ambassadeur, the Queen your
Mistress shall have me in her hands to do her will of me; and if
she be so hard-hearted as to desire my end, she may then do her
pleasure, and make sacrifice of me; peradventure that casualty
might be better for me than to live. In this matter, God's will be
fulfilled.

The queen of Scots' spirit of adventure, burnished by the grief
of her intense losses over the past year—the king, her childhood
friends to marriages, her mother, her husband, her throne and
future and now the country she loved so much (in fact nearly everything)—released her to what some might think an almost suicidal,
devil-may-care attitude, but what may in fact have been a deepening detachment and at the same time a deepening understanding of
her own destiny. She left security, comfort, elegance and devotion
to face uncertainty, discomfort, uncouthness and the distrust of a
large segment of her subjects.

Elizabeth's offer of safe-conduct came too late to reach Mary
before her departure from her graceful life in France across the
angry sea to the dim twilight of the north, where there awaited her
a country "filled with restless and turbulent people, who would be
difficult to control." How much the fact that her mother had lost
her own life holding the throne of Scotland for her daughter played
in Mary's decision to give up all she knew, and risk everything, cannot be underestimated.

8

Adieu France!

Adieu France! Adieu France! Adieu donc, ma chere France . . .
Je pense ne vous revoir jamais plus.

—*Mary Queen of Scots*

ON AUGUST 14, 1561, two great galleys and two ships departed Calais, France for the six-hundred-mile voyage to Scotland. The long and tragic journey to Fotheringhay had begun.

The queen's majestic galley, all white with gold gilding, and billowing sails shimmering silvery in the moon, glided quietly through the satiny dark waters, manned by fifty oarsman, twenty-five oars to a side. Mary forbade their whipping. She could not bear violence of any kind for any reason, and most especially not on her account. The second and smaller galley was red and carried two flags: a blue one with the arms of France aloft, and a white one at the stern.

As long as the coast of France was in sight, Mary remained at the stern. No longer able to keep up her elegant composure, she wept the tears she had bravely held back for so long. "Adieu France! Adieu." Somehow she knew she would never be coming back. As if to confirm her foreboding, a fishing boat sank in the harbor as they waited to embark, and all hands drowned. All aboard the queen's galley watched helplessly. The mists in the harbor lingered as though in mourning for the imminent loss of their fairytale queen.

Barely sixty passengers in all set sail. Accompanying Mary on her galley were three of her uncles; the Four Maries, her companions since infancy, who had sailed with her to France thirteen years before; and an entourage of French and Scottish noble ladies and gentlemen, willing to brave such a trip for Mary's sake. She was afforded little protection, besides their devotion. As if symbolic of the precarious life awaiting her, Mary crossed the seas utterly vulnerable, with neither French nor Scottish troops to shield her from harm. This was her choice. The naïvete of the gallant buffer she was offered by her devotees is indicated by the poet Bantome's reflecttion on the necessity of the ship's lantern: "Surely there be no need of that light to guide us over the sea. The sweet eyes of our Queen are bright enough to illumine all the ocean with their dazzling fires, nay, to set it in flames if need be."

The anticipated danger of Elizabeth intercepting their voyage came to nothing. According to William Cecil, Elizabeth's closest advisor: "The Queen's majesty's ships, that were upon the seas to cleanse them of pirates, saw her and saluted her galleys; and staying her ships, examined them of pirates, and dismissed them gently. One Scottish ship they did detain, as vehemently suspected of piracy."

Although she could not have known, Mary was in far greater peril from two men traveling with her on her galley than from anything the hazardous seas could bring upon her. And they were in equal danger of her, for in the dim future their intense desires to sway her fate in their favor would cause them to die miserably for love or lust of her.

One, a tender and gentle poet, the Frenchman Chatelard, was so helplessly and obsessively in love with Mary, he abandoned his wife for his platonic ardor, much like in the tradition of the troubadours. His behavior was entirely accepted, as poets and their flights of fancy were indulged and encouraged by the French court. Tragically, in Protestant Scotland, a poet's courtly love would be called scandalous.

For the other man, of whom it was doubtful she now took much notice during their crossing, Mary would forfeit everything—her crown, her kingdom, her son and her freedom. He, on the other hand, would suffer a horribly prolonged death in a Danish dungeon. James Hepburn, earl of Bothwell, twenty-five at the time of the voyage, in a few short but intense years would come to be seen as an enigma as much as Mary for all that befell them both. "Stubborn red hair, cropped close, covered his massive head, and a great war-like beak of a nose overshadowed a mouth of enormous width and a heavy jaw." His shoulders were broad and his body strongly built and compact. In contrast, his hands and feet were exceptionally fine and aristocratic. Reared in the French court, Bothwell was no boor as his enemies viewed him. He was fully conversant with all the graces of his time, which is important to keep in mind given Mary's future actions. His bearing was gallant, but a violent passion and overbearing defiance marred his elegance. His magnetic force, the equal of Mary's in many ways, dominated the love of many women.

Even as she tried to make the best of her situation as the seas carried her to her new life, Mary was severely depressed during the trip. On Tuesday, August 19, while her galley slipped silently through a not unexpected dense easterly fog the Scots call "haar" down the Firth of Forth and into the harbor at Leith, Mary was informed after the fact that they had been in great danger of being lost upon the rocks. For her own sake, Mary replied, if only for feeling sorry for Scotland if she died, there was nothing she would have welcomed more than death. However, so true to her nature, she rallied herself as the shores of Scotland drew close.

All aboard, except Mary, saw the dense fog that had accompanied them on the journey as a gloomy augury for the young queen. Jumping on any opportunity for a negative spin, Knox saw the heavy mists as an omen, a symbol of the "sorrow, dolour, darkness and impiety which the Queen was bringing to Scotland."

PEOPLE OF THE SIXTEENTH CENTURY, like indigenous people of today, looked to nature and the supernatural for clues to life's course. For them, life was expected to be short and beset with dangers. In the sixteenth-century's prevailing assumptions about reality, human nature and the place of men and women in the great hierarchy, all was believed to be linked with the Divine.

It was an era defined by the conflicts between great opposing forces: the Romanticists of the Renaissance versus the Puritan movement of the Protestant Reformation, with its "radical, uncompromising view of the human condition: nothing short of absolute commitment to godliness must be tolerated, and no accommodations must ever be made to Satan"; and, champions and defenders of feudal privileges and the Divine Right of Kings versus those who demanded popular liberties and individual freedom.

A precarious stage had been set for Mary's return. Her gilded galley dropped anchor on the shores of a country that had for a very long time been through the horrors of a civil war. The Catholic and Apostolic faith that was hers from birth was now overthrown. The religious adamancy of her realm would never abide her worldview. Yet, no new order had emerged from the political and religious chaos. It was a mad world she was entering. Public morale was at a low ebb. Jealous and intriguing nobles thought nothing of securing their own interests through treachery and assassination, a frequent handmaiden of diplomacy. Murder was as legitimate an instrument of political policy as marriage. "Clamorous people were roused to acts of violence by the tirades of ambitious demagogues."[1] Deprived of French support, Mary had few friends in Scotland.

Her subjects could not have been more different from the French, the only people she knew. The Scots were an "imaginative race, brave, simple, hardy and frugal. Hunting and fishing supplied their food. They flayed deer where it fell and the skin served as a vessel to hold water to boil the flesh. Wrapped in their plaids, they were the color of the heather among which they lurked. They braved the severest storms in the open air, sleeping sometimes in the snow."[2] The people were divided into mountaineer, borderer and lowlander. In the Western Highlands and on the islands, the people, divided into clans, were still of the Celtic faith. It was said that the Island Celts were pirates and the mainland Celts were thieves.

Mary faced governing a lawless realm, without help from the French and with virtually no trusted friends in Scotland. And cousin Elizabeth could hardly be called a friend. From his pulpit, John Knox was denouncing her as a "new Jezebel." Before leaving France, Mary regarded Knox as the most dangerous man in her dominions and was determined to banish him.

Yet under her rule, poor and undeveloped Scotland, though not a prize, was strategic, and played its greatest and most pivotal role ever in international diplomacy. France, England, Spain and the papacy, especially—all were watching with concern the fortunes of the Scottish queen. Her return to Scotland had the potential for enormous glory and success. Mary's personal policy with her realm of a half a million subjects was one of conciliation.

Favorable winds had created an earlier-than-anticipated arrival of the royal entourage. The local dignitaries were caught unprepared, and the Scottish lords had to be quickly notified. As word spread, the people rushed to witness the spectacle of their eighteen-year-old queen's arrival. They were not coming out of respect, but from curiosity. The crown had done little for any of them but cause misery. They were a divided people now, looking to the chiefs of their many clans to govern them. In their jealousy and to gain money and supremacy, the chiefs had long exploited the weaknesses of their sovereigns.

As the apathetic crowd gathered, down the gilded ramp came the most enchanting creature. Tall, willowy and regal, it must have seemed their queen was floating toward them, sweeping the unsuspecting crowd up in her own personal magic: her flawless complexion, her wide and pure brow, the heavy-lidded luminous chestnut eyes and richly burnished gold hair framing a majestic yet sweet face whose ethereal beauty held the crowd spellbound. Mary greeted her subjects in her genuinely outgoing and warm manner. Her demeanor was one of maternal solicitude. The Catholic bishop of Ross commented that Mary "tendered her subjects so lovingly, as she would use herself toward them as a natural mother to her child." Her royal bearing and vast personal charm entranced the crowd and had to have had the effect of instantly elevating them, as they suddenly saw themselves in a different light. This extraordinarily glamorous woman was their queen after all, and as the ancient Celts knew, the energy of the ruler transforms the people in many ways, for good or ill.

As the queen of Scots slowly moved through the crowd, she paused many times to offer endearing remarks to the townsfolk and

The Percys (the later dukes of Northumberland) backed
Mary Queen of Scots and now have her pincushion and hairnet
made of her own hair.
(Photo by Eric Lessing/Art Resource, NY)

their children who lined the way. Her voice had a soft, rich, hypnotic quality and she spoke to them in their language, the language of her birth, which she never forgot. Whether or not she was dismayed over the conditions of her country and her people, she heroically expressed her delight over everything she saw.

After an impromptu lunch at the home of the provost of the town, enough nobles had been gathered for a cortege to her new place of residence, the palace of Holyrood in Edinburgh. The contrast between the splendor she was so accustomed to and the meager accouterments provided for her procession to Edinburgh got the best of her and her spirits were dampened a bit. Her own horses had been on the ship detained by the English, and the lot of little, rough-hackneyed, shabbily compared Scottish horses caused her to momentarily break down and weep at the sorry sight. She did, however, quickly gather herself, and resume her good cheer for the sake of all her subjects.

Although not quite to the standards of French palaces, Holyrood was still magnificent. Just on the outskirts of the city, it was surrounded by a wild and bleak countryside. Enclosed by a moat, the palace was reached by a drawbridge. Under her father's direction, French masons had renovated the towered and turreted palace transforming it into a jewel of the Scottish Renaissance. Conjoining the palace was the abbey of Holyrood. Mary established herself in the northwest corner of the palace. The Great Hall took up most of the first floor, which led to a beautiful, private chapel with a carved ceiling, painted friezes and a gold and scarlet royal pew, and to an anteroom with a beautiful heraldic painting on the ceiling.

That first night, Mary was serenaded under her window by nearly six hundred of her subjects who had fallen under her spell. By all accounts, the music was a wretched insult to the finely tuned and cultured ears of those in her entourage. Probably though, when their alarm passed, the humor of the situation was seen. Though most likely their musical abilities were equally horrifying to Mary, she praised the enthusiastic serenaders and encouraged them to continue their nocturnal entertaining the next night.

In contrast to the maladroit musical repertoire of her Scottish subjects Mary brought with her the voluptuous refinement of the French Renaissance, and the atmosphere of her court was sensuous and playful. Elaborate masques were held in which Mary also acted. Equestrian events often featured horsemen dressed as women. Almost every night, music, singing, dancing, card playing, entertainment of some kind was provided. Mary loved any excuse for merrymaking. As she always felt close to those who were her servants, many of whom had always been with her, fun was always at hand. One of Elizabeth I's diplomats to her court, Sir Thomas Randolph, was both mesmerized and repelled by the Scottish court of Mary Queen of Scots and called it "a carnival aflow with illusion and sensuality." "Devilish devices," he said, "are imagined upon. Entertainments continued with joy and mirth and marvelous sights and shows. Nothing is left undone either to fill our bellies, feed our eyes, or content our minds." (Much of the contemporary commentary on Mary's life and habits were made through similar lenses of Puritanism.)

In the midst of all the revelry, the queen of Scots remained a paragon of virtue and purity. Though she was worshiped by many men, scandal never touched Mary. It can be assumed that if there had been any, it would have been leapt upon and magnified; at least a few of her enemies kept a vigilant watch over her. Although the influence of the French court was strong, the sway of her grandmother Antoinette and her aunt the abbess was even stronger. Her piety was deeply felt. Ritual nurtured her soul, and she would carry tapers at Candlemas and participate in religious ceremony rather than be a mere spectator. On Maundy Thursday, she would wash the feet of the poor.

MARY STUART ARRIVED on the shores of her native country tolerant and accommodating of the religion of others. Unfortunately, on her first Sabbath in Scotland she was not afforded the same respect. Her half brother Lord James protected her right to hear Mass in her own private chapel as promised, but he literally stood guard by the sanctuary door to ensure it. The crowd outside shouted that the Mass' idol-worshiping priest should be put to death, and smashed candles and altar ornaments being carried to the chapel by servants. Inside, the chapel was fraught with tension as the terrorized priest proceeded to say Mass. No one could be certain whether or not the chapel would be stormed by the enraged zealots and all murdered.

The next day, Mary issued a proclamation affirming her stand on tolerance and declaring the penalty for interference of any choice of religious worship to be death. Naturally, the intention of the proclamation was to protect her own servants and the Catholics of her court, as well as to put the Protestants at ease.

The following Sunday, John Knox denounced the saying and hearing of Mass as more fearful to him than the invasion of ten thousand enemy troops. Where Mary's Mass was attended by only a few, Knox preached to a packed crowd. Immediately, the queen of Scots summoned Knox to come to Holyrood for a personal interview. She was inviting the author of the *First Blast of the Trumpet Against the Monstrous Regiment of Women*. Originally intended to defile Mary Tudor, in it Knox declared that "to promote any woman—those weak, frail, impatient, feeble and foolish creatures—to any form of rule was the subversion of good order, of all equity and justice, as well as being contrary to God and repugnant to nature."

Where the first half of the sixteenth century had been ruled by virile leaders—Charles V, Henry VIII, Francois I—the second half was ruled by women—Mary Tudor, Elizabeth I, Catherine de' Medici, Marie de Guise and Mary Stuart. The young queen, in summoning Knox, was also sending for the man who, more than any other, hastened her own mother's death. She awaited him in her audience chamber, the largest of the rooms in her royal suite. Her brother James was there as witness and guards stood by the door.

When Knox entered, as ready to do battle against the devil as any saint, his presence was a formidable force. The virtual embodiment of the Reformation, in a short time, this one man, now forty-seven years old, had wiped the slate clean of the past, replacing it with a completely new doctrine and an extraordinarily rigid discipline. "No timid respect for antiquity weakened him." Knox was carrying on the process of transformation from Medievalism begun by Martin Luther, who, in April 1521 at the Great Hall at Worms before panic-stricken princes of the court, flung in the face of the emperor his defiance of the medieval church, which he called the "rotting foundation upon which for hundreds of years the institutions of Europe had rested."

Knox's own weakness was a sheer lack of charity and magnanimity, along with a violent and relentless self-righteousness. He felt the death of an unjust ruler to be totally justified. His bitterness was reflected in his face. Narrow-minded, superstitious in his own way, he possessed a fiery zeal and an enormous amount of energy. Material wealth meant nothing to him. As intolerant and overbearing as the most assiduous pontiff, Knox's only desire was for spiritual dominion—everything else was worthless.

As expected, the meeting was an impasse. Knox, desiring nothing short of domination, was never going to find it with Mary, who had avowed her royal sovereignty from birth, and was not about to give it up to anyone, let alone this preacher. His intimidation, the first time in her life she had ever been spoken to with any lack of respect, brought her to tears at one point. She quickly recovered though, and attacked him for turning the Scots against her mother, and for his opinions regarding women rulers.

They heatedly discussed the issue of religion. Knox agreed to tolerate her, and told her he would "be as well content to live under your Grace as Paul was to live under Nero." He still, however, affirmed his belief in the right of a people to rise up against an unworthy ruler who opposed God's word—presumably as interpreted by Knox himself. Mary replied, "I perceive that my subjects shall obey you and not me; and shall do what they list and not what I command; and so must I be subject to them and not they to me." Knox replied that subjugation to his God would bring her everlasting glory. When Mary claimed her church to be the true church of God, Knox told her, "Conscience requireth knowledge. And I fear right knowledge ye have none." Defending herself, Mary informed him, "But I have both heard and read."

The only one not to be captivated by Mary's allure, Knox wrote to a friend after their meeting, "If there be not in her a proud mind, a crafty wit, and an indurate heart against God and His truth, my judgment faileth me. In communication with her, I espied such craft as I have not found in such age."

If Knox and his zealots were not thrilled with her presence in Scotland, the people rejoiced, and celebrated her official entry into Edinburgh with pageantry. Nearly twenty years had passed since there was a ruling sovereign among them. Mary's father, King James V, was known for his way with the common people, as was his father King James IV before him. Both went among the people in disguise, her father often as a simple farmer, to get a real sense of their lives.

When away from her castle, Mary would lay aside her state and would be continually in the open air, hunting, hawking and the like. Each year she visited a different outlying district. One district in particular was incredibly poor and food was scarce. Rather than insist on her usual comforts, Mary shared her countrymen's daily lot, endearing her to them. Mary had clearly inherited her father and grandfather's simplicity and genuine concern, and the people loved her. Her people felt themselves fortunate to have such a queen, the most celebrated beauty of the age.

EDINBURGH WAS A HANDSOME CITY, looking much like an anthill as it was situated along a mile-long ridge running east to west. The stone-paved main thoroughfare was a fourteen hundred-foot-wide corridor, barely half as broad as it was long, where priests, nobles, tradesmen, merchants and the general public all mingled and did their business with each other. Crooked alleyways branched off from the main root, and ended where the land dropped off. Narrow and tall hewn stone buildings, and staircases leading up to each individual residence, housed the population.

Dressed up as Moors in yellow taffeta, their faces and bodies blackened, fifty townsmen officially greeted their queen a week after her arrival. Four beautiful virgins representing the four virtues greeted her further along the route at Tolbooth. Four more virgins, dressed to appear from heaven, were further down at Cross. Wine flowed abundantly for everyone. A pointed allegorical greeting awaited even further down the route. A child dressed as an angel descended from a globe suspended high above the street and handed Mary a Protestant Bible and Psalter along with the keys to the city. Threaded throughout the crowd were signs and banners declaring "The Vengeance of God Upon Idolaters." A child was set up to ask that she put aside the Mass. Fortunately, plans to burn a priest saying Mass in effigy were scrapped. The lavishness of her welcome irritated Knox enormously and he remarked that in their farces, masks and other prodigalities, "fain would the fools have counterfeited France."

Three weeks after arriving in Holyrood, Mary set out on a tour of some of her realm. Her first stop was the palace of Linlithgow, the place of her birth. She then went onto Stirling, where a flame from a candle set fire to the curtains by her bed while she slept. The fire was quickly put out, and she escaped unharmed. During High Mass at the castle's chapel royal, Lord James and the earl of Argyll, a leading Protestant, lost control of themselves and began fighting with the choir, leaving a few priests and some of the clerks banged up and bloody. Mass continued.

At each stop, there were scattered protests by Protestants, but for the most part, everyone treated her with great honor. At Perth, one protest was so offensive that Mary fell ill, nearly fainting in the street, and had to be carried off her horse to a nearby dwelling. She was prone to nervous collapse after being subjected to any sort of great unkindness or grief. The culmination of protests and the constant need to adapt to harsher situations than she had ever encountered took its toll; but as always, Mary recovered her high spirits quickly. She went on to Dundee and then St. Andrews, where the next Sabbath a priest was slain. After a quick stop at Falkland Palace, Mary returned to her primary residence at Holyrood on September 29.

Knox must have held some expectations of the impact of her trip through Protestant territory. Still unable to grasp that she could make a distinction between private devotion and public policy, he felt she was unmoved from her "devilish opinions" after her journey, despite the protests of the Protestants that greeted her along the way. For herself, Mary was more certain than ever that the status quo needed to be preserved. She only wished for their loyalty to her as sovereign.

With Mary's presence in Scotland, Catholics had become bolder and more public again, and many not-so-zealous Protestants were more malleable. Naturally the extremists tried to suppress this trend, and on the second of October, the town council of Edinburgh proclaimed priests to be in the same category as prostitutes and whoremongers. As more subjects were aligned with her, she was able to suppress the proclamation. On All Hallow's Day, it was decided that indeed the queen was entitled to hear Mass in private, although the singing that could be heard out in the courtyard was still a sore spot.

In December the pope wrote Mary that she should be taking the example of Mary Tudor as her guide, the Catholic queen who had ruthlessly terrorized and executed thousands of Protestants. Although it could be argued, and has been stated, that Mary refused the pope's wishes solely because of her drive to procure Elizabeth's acknowledgement of her right to succession of the English throne, it is highly doubtful, given her peace-loving nature and extreme sensitivity, that, were succession to the throne of Protestant England not an issue, she would have enforced her faith on her subjects. Nothing in her behavior thus far in her life indicates she could be such a zealot, no matter how strong her convictions.

Given that she could not tolerate even the normal whipping of oarsmen on her voyage to Scotland, it is hard to imagine Mary could allow torture and murder in the name of anything. Although she could not have been unaware of the ruthless policies of her Guise uncles, she chose to be tender in her ways just as her mother had been, unless forced by her enemies to do battle. It seems it would have been impossible for her to be any other way, and so, despite being now only nineteen, she could confidently defy the pope's wishes.

ALTHOUGH ALREADY KNOWN FOR her courage in France, the depth of her bravery only became apparent in Scotland, where it was needed in serious situations, rather than just being useful for the hunt. Mary was a fearless and indefatigable rider and could gallop ninety miles without changing horses. She thrilled to the excitement of the chase, whether hawking or deer hunting, a favorite pastime of royalty for centuries. She joined in battles against her enemies and in one foray against Lord Huntley, she was overheard to say she wished she were a man, "to know what life it was to lie all night in the field, or to watch on the cawsey with a Glasgow buckler and a broad sword."

In a female ruler this quality of daring and bravery, combined with her fine mind and intense femininity, was exceptionally potent in rallying men to her side and causing them to fall head over heels for her. Within the first six months of Mary's arrival, twice plots to abduct her were uncovered (one by the man Bothwell, who later would himself abduct her and become her husband). Her Guise relations had left after seeing her settled, and it was her half brother Lord James to whom she could look the most for protection. In one plot, she was the object of the obsessive love of a madman, Arran, a contender for the throne, and in the other, the pawn in a passionately long-held dispute between two rival families.

Besides being a vulnerable political pawn, Mary Stuart was captivating. Girl as she was, she was hardly inferior in intellectual power to Elizabeth I herself, while "in fire and grace and brilliancy of temper she stood high above her." Where Elizabeth was seen as "more than man and less than woman," Mary was seen to have "a finer poise—a truer balance, all the charm of a woman, with much of the strength of a man—of a daring man and a bewitching woman."

Many male writers especially did not know in what context to put her feminine power, and preferred to make it sexual, blaming her for their reactions to her, and for their fear that their own will would be seduced by her powers. Protestant writers depicted her as a "scheming seductress and bloodthirsty competitor" for Elizabeth's crown.

"In her writings, as in her acts, we see the passionate woman avid for enjoyment, and resentful of anything that deprived her of the sensuous delight of life. The plaintiff beauty who appeals to the pity of men, in sorrow and distress, wields the most powerful weapon in the feminine armory; and when her claim is only youth and loveliness should be happy, her fascination is irresistible."[3]

"Surely she was a high kind of woman, with haughty energies most flashing, fitful discernments; generosities; too fitful all, though most gracefully elaborated; the born daughter of heroes—but sore involved with papistries, French coquetries, poor woman; and the dash of gypsy tragic in her I doubt not; and was seductive enough to several, instead of being divinely beautiful to all. Considering her grand rude task in this world, and her beautiful, totally inadequate faculty for doing it, even Dryasdust has felt that there was seldom anything more tragical."[4]

"Her beauty, her exquisite grace of speech, her sensibility, her gaiety, her womanly tears, her man-like courage, the play and freedom of her nature, the flashing poetry that broke from her at every intense moment of her life, flung a spell over friend or foe which has only deepened with the lapse of years."[5]

Even after being imprisoned and rendered impotent, Mary was seen as a "scheming and seductive witch." Her tears softened hearts; her graciousness jeopardized Elizabeth.

Despite her flagrant affairs, Elizabeth I was able to detach herself from the corporal in the mind of her subjects and fulfilled her desire to be known as the Virgin Queen, "the pure mother of her country, offering herself up as mother to all without a husband, without sexual guilt—that mythic point of origin by which her subjects need not feel complicated or corrupted."[6] Ironic that, as her country rejected Catholicism and its intrinsic worship of the patriarchal Virgin Mary, the mother who conceived without sex, Elizabeth fulfilled that role for them.

"Once the Goddess had been overthrown, and her cult vilified, it was easy in patriarchal understanding to turn the sacred harlot in the service of the Goddess into an abominable seductress."[7] With the unconscious embodiment of the lost feminine of ancient times, which included the worship of sexuality and the feminine arts, Mary was reviled at the same time that she enthralled all who rejected that part of themselves. She was the forbidden mother, the mother who enjoyed all of life and its abundance—a dangerous woman, far too dangerous to go unchecked.

9

Her Scottish Court

As EARLY AS 1560, the Spanish ambassador de Quandra observed about the English: "The cry is that they do not want any more women rulers." Beyond being another female ruler, Mary Queen of Scots, as possible successor to the English throne, was an especially unpopular choice given she was considered a French woman, and the English dreaded being absorbed by France through her; she also was related to the Guises and she was Catholic.

There was something else, too: the English Parliament, with its Puritan leanings, could not tolerate the idea of dealing with the "uncontainable erotic power that made Mary so dangerous." But ensuring her succession to the English throne was all-consuming to Mary, to the point of being a lifelong obsession.

Whether this would have been as much an obsession if she were more ambiguously next in line, as Lady Catherine Grey or her future mother-in-law, Countess Margaret of Lennox were, is an important question with regard to Mary's motives, character and the choices she made that propelled her to the executioner's block. Much has always been made about how driven Mary was to succeed to the English throne. She fought for it right up until the end of her life. The two nearest contenders to Mary were English, as Henry VIII had stipulated was a prerequisite, and related through the same great grandfather as Mary, Henry VII, but not as directly.

Was Mary fighting her whole life for what she felt was verifiably rightfully hers and unable because of her imperious nature to give it up on principal? Was she being prodded still by her uncles in their bid for more power, or by the Catholics as some would believe? Did she have a huge appetite for power, an unquenchable ambition? Or was it true, as Sir Frances Knollys, one of her jailers, said of her:

> The thing she most thirsteth after is victory, so that for victory's sake, pain and peril seem pleasant to her, and in respect to victory, wealth and all things seem to her vile and contemptible. Surely she is a rare woman, for as no flattery can lightly abuse her, no plain speech seemeth to offend her, if she think the speaker thereof be an honest man.

How Mary is viewed as a ruler and a woman depends on which motivation is attributed to her, and the interpreter's own bent.

Mary Stuart was of a much finer and nobler nature than Elizabeth, possessing a higher courage, greater conviction and generosity. She was far more magnanimous, a more fascinating beauty and brighter. The equal of Elizabeth, she was a cool and astute politician. However, Mary did not have Elizabeth's caution and love of mastery, which were Elizabeth's safeguards. Some believed Mary Stuart's relentless ambition for the English throne "warped her goodness, made her a hapless plaything for her cunning enemies, and ruined the religious cause she loved better than her life."

Learning that safe-conduct had been given for her voyage to Scotland after all, Mary began her campaign for succession again in earnest with a heavy letter-writing and gift-giving campaign. All Mary ever wanted to do was meet Elizabeth. Well aware of her own enormous powers of persuasion, Mary knew in her heart if she were given an audience with her cousin, the issue of succession would be settled. "We are both in one isle, both of one language, both the nearest kinswoman that each other hath, and both Queens." Mary often joked that the issue would be settled swiftly if only one of them were a man. Sir Nicholas Throckmorton, so much an admirer of Mary's after she became a widow, had already wished the same, perhaps first to Mary. "Methinketh it were to be wished of all wise men and her Majesties' good subjects, that one of these two Queens of the Ile of Britain were transformed into the shape of a man to make so happy a marriage, as thereby there might be an unitie of the whole and their appendances."

Despite the protests of her subjects and Parliament, Mary was Elizabeth's first choice of all the succession candidates. The problem was that Elizabeth was reluctant to name any successor, as she was certain her life would then forever be in danger and any dealings with her successor would always be suspect. "The desire is without example to require me in mine own life, to set my winding sheet before my eyes. Think you I could love my own winding sheet? Princes cannot like their own children, those that should succeed unto them." As if naming a successor would be at the same time crowning one, Elizabeth understood the "inconstancy of the people of England, how they ever mislike the present government and have their eyes fixed upon that person next to succeed. They are more prone to worship the rising than the setting sun."[1]

Not only had Elizabeth witnessed such capricious loyalty in her subjects, her own mother lost her life to her father's fickle nature. If Mary could have seen beyond her own ambition and understood Elizabeth's deeply held and understandable fears, she may have avoided becoming the reenactment of the English queen's early childhood trauma and her head may have remained with her body.

"For so long as I shall live, there shall be no queen in England but I," Elizabeth I declared to William Maitland, Mary's talented ambassador, sent to England thirteen days after her arrival in Scotland to plead for right of succession. Elizabeth saw things clearly, without bitterness and without illusion, so accustomed was she from childhood to seeing how little loyalty meant in the face of opportunity.

Her discussions with Maitland revealed her practicality. "As children dream in their sleep of apples, and in the morning when as they wake and find not the apples . . ." So every man who pressed her with flattery in hopes of gaining favor and not receiving it, looked to new possibilities. "No princes' revenues be so great that they are able to satisfy the insatiable cupidity of men," she told him. When she argued that Mary, "being a puissant princess and so near our neighbor, her subjects may love me, but not with complete contentment," Maitland tried to reassure her. But Elizabeth would not be impressed. "It is hard to bind princes by any security where hope is offered of a kingdom."

While in private and informally she could consider Mary her rightful heir, Elizabeth would not make it official. Maitland was to continue negotiations with Sir William Cecil under the supervision of their respective queens. Elizabeth did concede that Mary would not have to renounce her claim altogether as part of the Treaty of Edinburgh. Returning to Scotland hopeful, Maitland reported to Mary that there was interest on Elizabeth's part to meet her. Mary was thrilled, and continued her personal correspondence with Elizabeth. At one point she wrote: "If God will grant a good occasion that we may meet together, which we wish may be soon, we trust you shall more clearly perceive the sincerity of our good meaning than we can express by writing."

As a token of her friendship, Mary sent Elizabeth a heart-shaped ring with a diamond in the design, along with poetry, which Mary loved to have accompany any gift. Elizabeth returned the favor with her own gift of a ring to Mary, which the queen of Scots, by one of her advisor's accounts, "marvelously esteemed, oftentimes looked upon, and many times kissed."

SIR WILLIAM MAITLAND of Lethington, Mary's most trusted advisor, was thought by Elizabeth to be "the flower of the wits of Scotland." Advisor first to her mother, Maitland, a handsome man of thirty-three, was a kindred spirit to Mary, great company and at the same time a great statesman. Together, Mary and Maitland were a new breed of thinkers. They "lacked fanatical fervour, held contempt for convention and conventional methods, and desired freedom from obsolete prepossessions. In their frankness and their urbanity, they were modern spirits."[2] Both desired to create an orderly government and worked toward the reorganization of a disorganized society of anarchic nobles and arrogant priests. Maitland was a natural leader, a scholar in keeping with Mary, but he was a gambler to his undoing. His restless nature abhorred a steady course; this restlessness, and his need for drama to thrive, undermined his ability to handle the fierce and lawless nobles for Mary. Treason, schemes and murder kept him intrigued. Exceptionally self-serving, he was charming despite it all. "Had he possessed less talent and more honesty, he and his country would have been better off. He could have been a great asset to many." Tragically for Mary, he wasn't.

Through the year and into the spring, Maitland continued to negotiate for a face-to-face meeting between the queens. To the Scottish Parliament, cost was a huge consideration as was Mary's safety, given less than a year before Elizabeth I had threatened their queen before her voyage over. Scottish Protestants were pleased and worried at the prospect—pleased that Mary would lean more toward them and worried that Elizabeth would cease protecting them with quite such care. The Catholics out-and-out did not want a meeting to happen, since they were already feeling ignored by their Catholic queen. However, Mary was not so much ignoring them as being conscious of her place in the coming struggle between freedom and authority in religion. In the end, Mary's will prevailed, and Maitland arrived back in London on May 31 for further negotiations.

Mary wrote to Elizabeth to show the "bottom of her mind nakedly": "Whereon the matter being so knit up, and the seed of dissension uprooted, we shall present to the world such an amity as has never been seen." Beyond the hunger for power always attributed as the reason she fought so hard for succession, the idealistic Mary Queen of Scots may have held a vision of peace for their world, made by two women, as opposed to the brutal politics she had witnessed all of her life. Mary was ready to put herself in Elizabeth's hands, confident in the English queen's "uprightness and judgment." Mary trusted Elizabeth as if they were sisters, and "loveth her as entirely."

Negotiations went forward, despite Elizabeth's ambassador Cecil's private concerns that two such different women meeting may cause more problems than if they never did. At Mary's still naïve and coddled stage, meeting "a woman of stinging eccentricity, who smelt of vinegar and was so eaten up with bitterness that she slapped and stabbed her waiting women and demanding they tell her she was beautiful; but was still capable of tenderness, may have been a recipe for disaster. Daily, Elizabeth swore her favorite oath, 'God's death!,' and swung a rusty old sword."[3] Her moods were radically unpredictable.

If the cost wasn't prohibitive, the excessively rainy weather that summer made a meeting nearly impossible. However, negotiations reached such a point where three nights of masques to entertain the two queens were already being planned. The allegorical theme selected was the Punishment of False Report and Discord by Jupiter at the request of Prudence and Temperance.

Extreme care was being taken to ensure neither queen would be by any means slighted. Unfortunately, just when the meeting appeared certain to happen, "Prudence and Temperance" had abandoned France, ironically since Mary's own uncles were deeply involved, and the French Huguenots and Catholics were at civil war with each other. Though both queens were ready to abandon their opposing loyalties, it became too dangerous for either to travel and Elizabeth canceled their summer meeting. On finding out, Mary collapsed in a deluge of tears and took to her bed for the rest of the day.

But she was consoled that Elizabeth wanted to meet within a year. The potential of such an historic meeting to forever change the destiny of both countries, especially England, and the fates of both queens, especially Mary, has inspired playwrights, poets and authors through the centuries to speculate about what would have actually transpired between the two women had they ever met. Fate, which had given Mary so many gifts, denied her the opportunity to use them when she needed them most. If Elizabeth had ever met Mary, and been seduced like all the rest by her extraordinary charms, it is highly doubtful it would have come to pass that she would have imprisoned her dear cousin for half her life before finally signing her death warrant.

"ENGLAND UNDER ELIZABETH I was a brilliant pageant centered on the queen and her courtiers, her soldiers and explorers, her poets and scholars."[4] Mary was not an obsession for her. The Scottish queen's monarchy was quite poor, though Mary did all she could to recreate some of the lavishness of the French court, as was expected of monarchs. In a tradition based on ancient esoteric teachings and carried on if not begun by the troubadours from the eleventh to fourteenth centuries, the royal court of a country was to provide for the arts so that the whole country benefited by the uplifting of the spirit. The original band of troubadours numbered around four hundred and they were active among the monarchies of France, Spain and Italy. Their secret purpose was to disseminate, through the arts, ideals of virtue, good manners, kindness and courage in order to ultimately bring about the universal reformation of mankind and their hope for a world democracy. They policed the abuses of the Church and defended the oppressed. Many members of the upper classes became troubadours and traveled to courts and castles spreading their teachings called "Courts of Love."

Disguised as romantic passion their poems, songs and literature were really about the Divine love God has for humans. Their purpose was to empower individuals with that understanding, as opposed to the Church's intention to subjugate the faithful, which is why the troubadours were nearly wiped out during the Inquisition. When the troubadours sang and wrote their passionate ballads to the lady of their heart, or to their queen, their true "lady" was a particular goddess or the goddess.

Given the renewed infusion of esoteric teachings during the Renaissance, it is very possible that some of the poets of the courts of France, England and Scotland were of that secret tradition. Whether Mary or Elizabeth consciously understood that the praise they received was really for the soul of their countrymen, they were always being personally uplifted by the efforts. Mary Stuart's innately mystical and lively nature was especially receptive.

The source of this tradition may have become obscured, but certain customs endured. No country wanted to boast of an impoverished monarchy, so it was important to put on a show. On May 26, 1563, Mary officially rode to Parliament, "the solemnity whereof hath been very great." The queen wore her Parliamentary robes and a "very fair rich crown upon her head." Following the men were thirty-two women, including the Four Maries, who were damsels of honor. By one account, "A fairer sight was never seen, women so wonderful in beauty as to be incomparable in any court."

Mary was resilient by nature and able to make merriment where there appeared to be none. Few in Scotland could provide the mental stimulation that the French court could, and Mary's own court imported musicians, poets and entertainers from Europe, especially France. Her library was the most extensive in all of Scotland. Knox felt her court was more like a brothel, especially because he could not tolerate her dancing. His public condemnation of the pleasure she took in it caused her to demand a second interview with her to set him straight.

Her enjoyment of and craving for the outdoors, the wildness of nature and the beauty of formal gardens supplied much of her entertainment. On a trip through the hauntingly beautiful Highlands, Elizabeth's diplomat Sir Thomas Randolph observed that he had never seen her so happy. While at her various castles, the gardens were frequently used for political audiences, and in her love of fresh air, she once even held a meeting in the garden at Holyrood in February. She brought over a young sycamore tree from France, from which originated the celebrated sycamore groves in Scottish ballads.

Mary's ardent nature and her exuberant love of life and intense love of pleasure drew admirers like moths to a flame. "Unlike Elizabeth, she did not hector her lovers into a condition of maudlin ecstasy, but inspired them willingly or unwillingly with a passion so strong that it overcame fear and made them bold."[5] Elizabeth, on the other hand, "never allowed her slaves to assume the slightest liberty or overt familiarity on the strength of her passing fancy for them." Many found it impossible to understand how Mary could enjoy herself and flirt with such light-hearted abandon and not be a "strumpet."

Gallant, handsome and aristocratic Pierre de Chatelard, one of the most fashionable of the court poets of the Ronsard school, felt anything but platonic toward his queen. Mary openly flirted with him, but had no serious interest. She assumed it was play. "Of what use," he challenged her, "is it to possess wide spreading domains, cities, crowns, and bowing people, to be admired, respected, feared, and gazed at and yet sleep alone in glacial widowhood?" Twice he was discovered in Mary's bedchamber to the queen's horror. The second time he unnerved her so much that when her brother, James, entered her chamber after hearing her hysterical cries, she asked that he kill Chatelard then and there on the spot. James calmed his sister, and Chatelard was hauled off to the dungeons of St. Andrews and, after a public trial, was executed on February 22. Chatelard, discovered to be a Huguenot, confessed and rumor already had it that he had been set up to defame Mary by a Frenchman. However, Chatelard's dying words were to Mary: "Adieu, the most beautiful and the most cruel princess in the world."

To have a lovesick subject executed was an amazingly severe reaction on Mary's part, and the first time ever she was directly responsible for the death of another. Given her abhorrence of violence, her great love of poetry and poets and loyalty to friends, her immediate reaction to have Chatelard executed after discovering him in her room may have been the turning point that allowed all the tragedy that would soon befall her. Such a dramatic change in character indicates a disturbance had been developing.

Mary began her journey to Scotland under a threat by one of the darkest and most dangerous of the nobles, James Earl of Morton, to put Mary to death within three hours of her landing in Scotland. Morton's rivals, it was known, died like flies. It was believed that not even God with support behind him could have withstood him.

During his time as regent of Scotland, Morton's atrocities included the hanging of women still holding their babes in their arms. He drove prisoners to the gallows like sheep, piercing them through with spears as they ran. Mary could quite naturally have felt tremendously afraid for her life by Chatelard's unexpected actions. Several serious abduction attempts had already been made that were dangerous threats to her well-being, if not her life. Already she had witnessed a great deal of violence in the name of politics. She could have already heard the rumors of Chatelard setting her up before his bold penetration into her bedchamber. If he were part of a conspiracy, there must have appeared to her to be only one way to end it and send a message to any others.

Some, however, attributed her reaction to extreme prudishness. Prudishness seemed to be a trait of Mary's. Or else, what seemed like prudishness was really self-preservation. As a woman and a queen, she was extremely vulnerable. If she was to be abducted and raped and consequently became pregnant with the heir to the throne, she would lose all of her power and be forced to be subject to someone not at all of her choosing.

But for Mary to be responsible for another's death, especially someone not a clear enemy, had to mean, given her compassionate and sensitive nature, that she would be forever changed.

WITHIN THE NEXT TWO WEEKS, Mary learned of the death of two of her Guise uncles, one murdered, which, combined with the execution of Chatelard, had her completely undone. Elizabeth's advisor Randolph remarked that though Mary shed "manie a salte teare," most people he knew were overjoyed at her uncles' deaths. "I never saw merrier hearts with heavier looks since I was born."

A letter from Elizabeth consoled her and caused her to increasingly value the need for their friendship. Mary Fleming slept with her in her room, after Chatelard had entered so easily. But the recent incidents caused her to remark to Randolph, "I see now that the world is not that that we do make of it, nor yet are they most happy that continue longest in it."

Everything suddenly seemed too much to bear for the twenty-one-year-old widow, whose naturally bounteous spirit was struggling in such a rough and puritanical country. At a low point, she wrote to her uncle, Cardinal Lorraine, to tell him of her "wretchedness in this miserable country, and [her] determination if possible to remedy the evils in it, if necessary at the cost of [her] own life, which [she] would deem [herself] happy to sacrifice rather than change [her] faith or approve of any of their heresies." But even her uncle soon let her down, as she was forced to bitterly observe that he could not really have cared less about her needs except for what her marriage could provide for his own self.

Throughout the autumn of 1563, Mary suffered from what almost seemed like manic depression, weeping uncontrollably one moment and then suddenly bursting with merriment. Her physician modified her diet. Along with the recent political murders and executions she had to endure that were so against her nature, stress over her marriage prospects undoubtedly exacerbated her condition. A widow, now four years, Mary, though hardly desperate, needed to become realistic about her prospects.

Chatelard's words about her "glacial widowhood" may have also hit the mark emotionally. Unlike her cousin Elizabeth the Virgin Queen, who could not endure the idea of another commanding her and insisted on being both queen and king, Mary was more suited to having a companion with whom to rule. Her first choice continued to be the wretched, by now completely insane Don Carlos of Spain, who would hardly be able to satisfy anything but her ambitions, and had no capacity to be a companion to her.

Given that she had been raised so strictly Catholic, and her first husband had been more a boy, Mary had yet to experience sexual passion. She loved weddings and always became extremely involved in the planning for her friends'. She had a romantic nature. Perhaps, though, she had learned to accept her fate that she would have a loveless marriage. If she were to choose her own husband, it would mean she would be choosing on her own a leader for her people, instead of the king being chosen by the country's advisors, and approved of by the leaders of the countries most affected. She insisted from the beginning on making her own decision under the guidance of her advisors.

There were a great many considerations in the choice of a new husband. Foremost to Mary was to marry a Catholic, which would automatically offend her country, half of France and nearly all of England. Catholic Spain would be happy, though. England and France, however, had reason to worry about a Scottish alliance with Spain. There seemed no solution that would make everyone happy, although everyone gave their input, including Knox, whose admonitions of Mary from the pulpit continued to escalate and cause her much affliction.

The most outrageous suggestion for a prospective groom, and the most delicate to decline, came from Elizabeth I. Lord Robert Dudley, Elizabeth's best and oldest friend and lover, whom she would have married herself if she had ever desired to take a husband, was proffered as first choice. Elizabeth went so far as to name Dudley the earl of Leicester, a royal title making him a worthy husband for a queen and so more enticing to Mary. All attending the ceremony could not help noticing that Elizabeth touched the back of Dudley's neck with the deep affection of a lover. Ironically, the actual future husband of the queen of Scots, nineteen-year-old Henry Stuart, Lord Darnley, a grandson of Henry VIII's sister Margaret Tudor, carried the English queen's royal sword of honor during the procession for Dudley.

Given that Mary's first priority was to ensure succession to the English throne, she had to weigh Elizabeth's preferences more than any others. But many believed Dudley was not worthy to wipe Queen Mary's shoes. Elizabeth's motives for offering her lover and best friend had to have been pretty compelling. It would not be out of the realm of consideration that, should anything happen to Mary after her marriage to Dudley, he and Elizabeth could then marry and unite the two kingdoms themselves.

Finally Philip II ended any hopes of a union of his son with Mary. It was hard for Mary to let go of the possibility, though it is difficult to understand her reasoning at this stage. Perhaps she was craving the companionship of her childhood friend, Henri II's daughter Elizabeth, and the more refined atmosphere of the Spanish court, not to mention escape from the brutality of Scotland. But it was unlikely she would ever conceive a child with Don Carlos, who was now completely mad.

In December of 1563, Mary was bedridden with a severe pain in her right side, which from then on sporadically recurred throughout the rest of her life. One suggested cause was that she had danced excessively and well into the wee hours on her twenty-first birthday. Mary herself felt the pain was the result of praying far too long in an icy cold chapel. Perhaps it wasn't the icy cold chapel, but the prayers themselves. For to remain in an icy cold chapel to pray after Mass, much had to have been already weighing heavily on her mind, and, perhaps more importantly, on her soft-hearted conscience. Forced to become more and more detached from her own kind and feminine nature in order to survive among the savage nobles, so much so that now she was capable of allowing a lovesick poet to be put to death, Mary Stuart's true imprisonment may have already begun. Decisions she was to make from this point on took many disastrous turns, and shocked all who loved and admired her.

10

A Husband

She sought, with eyes still troubled by the storm,
The sky of purity, now far away,
Like a departed traveller who turns
To see the landscape he passed yesterday.
—*Charles Baudelaire*, from *Women Damned*

WHATEVER PRAYERS WERE LEFT in the ethers or absorbed by the frigid stones of her chapel royal, when Mary arose from her knees she left behind something deep within that had always nobly steered her course. A dark night of the soul was soon to befall her, undoing all the hope she had brought to her country.

The catalyst of her undoing crossed the border from England into Scotland on the eleventh of February in 1565, at a time of escalating frustration and disappointment for the Scottish queen. Taking everyone by surprise, Elizabeth I had given Henry Stuart, Lord Darnley, passport into Scotland. Some actually, at first, thought he was Robert Dudley, earl of Leicester. An extremely clever manipulator, Elizabeth never did anything without a motive. Her shrewd and agile mind was used always in service to herself, and was now called into service of her great need to surpass her rival and protect her throne.

Some say Elizabeth's weakness was that she could not make decisions at crucial times. Appearing not to make a decision kept her irreproachable and deflected any opposition, while at the same time, events moved along effortlessly on her behalf. This could not have been by accident all the time. Surely she knew Darnley's character well, and, as many came to believe, deliberately sent him to Mary as bait, in hopes of trapping the queen of Scots into a misalliance likely to bring her and her country nothing but unhappiness.

In the beginning, Mary did not rise to the lure. Darnley's refined appearance and graceful bearing, his ability to dance, play music, ride and hunt all made a good first impression on the Scottish court. Reared knowing he was within the shadow of the throne, as first prince of blood royal by right of birth, he presented himself as privileged, of the sacred royal caste. Always on the short list of possible grooms for his distant cousin the Scottish queen, and with an extraordinarily ambitious mother and power-hungry father who had once before promoted their son while Mary was still in France, Darnley could only be arriving in Scotland for the express purpose of winning the hand of the queen of Scots. The opportunity was there to go, in an instant, from obscurity into full power. Unfortunately, he had no vision other than prestige, and little strength of purpose other than that provided by his striving parents.

The nineteen-year-old Darnley met with Mary at the castle of the Laird of Wemyss on February 17. He stayed there a couple of days before meeting with his father, the earl of Lennox. As he strode forward to greet her, Mary had to have been delighted to be in the company of a man taller than herself, a man she could dance comfortably with and actually look up to—such a rare treat for her. His hair was golden and his perfectly shaped face was fair and smooth, so smooth as to be offensive and suspect to the more rugged Scots— a face more reminiscent for Mary of the French court. His beautiful hazel eyes were slanting, but offered little, and a hint of cruelty played about his Cupid-shaped lips. But this would not be noticed at first.

Though Mary enjoyed his company, she did not appear to be dazzled. She was sufficiently impressed with his physique, however, declaring that he was the "properest and best proportioned long man that ever she had seen." After meeting with his father, himself a gallant and extremely charming man of the court, Darnley rode back in time to enter Edinburgh with the queen, a gesture that could not have been uncalculated. He dined with her brother James, heard Knox preach and danced some more with the queen. Mary continued her perfect self-command. Determined again to enjoy life to its utmost, she confronted Randolph at a point when she could tell he was becoming exasperated by her procrastination on a few political matters. "I see how well you are weary of this company and treatment," she told him. "I sent for you to be merry and to see how like a burgess wife I live with my little troop, and you will interrupt our pastimes with your grave matters."

As much as Mary loved to enjoy good times, she never before allowed anything to ultimately interfere with her aims as ruler of Scotland. Darnley might be able to aid her slightly with Elizabeth with regard to succession, but he would upset many of the lords who despised the Lennox-Stuarts, and this mattered to Mary. Old feuds and animosities would surely be rekindled. So, Mary Stuart enjoyed Darnley's company, glad to have another around who also pursued pleasure with the same intensity, but she paid little real attention to him. She did not notice his lack of inclination for reflection, his weak moral character, his arrogance and petulance, his hatred of criticism and great instability. Darnley was excessively spoiled and the world revolved solely for him. These characteristics, however, did not get put to the test during the festivities of the court. They would not have been noticed.

In what had to have been carefully timed with Darnley's appearance at the Scottish court, Elizabeth informed Mary that a marriage to Dudley, now the earl of Leicester, would not guarantee succession to her throne. This was crushing news to Mary, despite the fact that Elizabeth's offer of her infamous horse keeper was insulting. Mary resented being held in suspense for so long and for nothing, and would find it hard to trust Elizabeth again. Her dream of a great Spanish match was permanently crushed, and she had been abandoned, by his own impotence, by her uncle the cardinal of Lorraine.

At some point, despairing of finding a husband that was her equal, Mary must have turned to Darnley with different eyes. He was a Catholic and was himself in line of succession to the English throne. Grandson of Margaret Tudor, first wife of King James IV, by her second marriage to Archibald Earl of Angus, through his mother, he was connected with fourteen kings and queens. Still no passion was in evidence.

At the court, two of her Maries were getting married. Mary Livingstone, the first bride, wed a younger son of Lord Sempel. The recently widowed Maitland, forty-four, was dazzled and delighted by Mary Fleming, now twenty-two. Reporting to Catherine de' Medici, the French ambassador said of Mary, "She has begun to marry off her Maries, and says that she wishes she herself were of the band."

As a welcomed addition to the court, Darnley became Mary's constant companion. The lords were beginning to be worried that they were losing some control of Mary: "You know her years, you see the lustiness of her boddie." However, the longer Darnley stayed at the court, the more many wondered if this "fair and jolly young man" was fit for high position.

It was not until Darnley became ill in April with the measles that their passion flared. As the frequency of her visits to his bedside to nurse him increased, so did her feelings for her patient. In the intimacy of the sickroom at Stirling, the soft breezes of spring fanning the flames, romance blossomed. This was the wild card that no one could control: "the uncontrollable if transient, passion of an ardent young woman for a particular man."

Overwhelmed by such unexpected and overpowering feelings, Mary completely lost her head. Four years of exemplary rule were washed away by the tide of her emotions for Darnley. Falling head over heels was not the problem. It was that she did not see that "beneath the surface of this tall, handsome princeling, with his pretty manners and courtly accomplishments, lay a spoilt, loutish, unstable youth with all the makings of a vindictive bully."[1] But love can be blind, and Darnley was like a drug. He blotted out all the pain, the wounds to her refined and sensitive soul at the hands of the ruthless nobles. Mary had not yet discovered that she was voluntarily welcoming abuse into her own bedchamber, although everyone around her, including her beloved confidants, the Four

Maries, were very much against the match.

Almost immediately upon winning her heart, Darnley's once-affable nature became "insufferable in his willful arrogance." He began to control and command Mary. Once he nearly killed one of his allies with a dagger when the man brought a message from the queen that he did not like. Clearly he was suddenly over his head and, there was little doubt, unprepared to assume such power.

Randolph was so profoundly shocked by the change he had seen in Mary and by her reckless behavior, her "pitiful and lamentable" state, that he thought she could literally have been bewitched. (It was a common practice in Scotland to put a spell on someone.) "She who had been so worthy, so wise, so honorable in all her doings hath now so altered with affection for Lord Darnley, that she hath brought her honor into question, her estate in hazard, and her countrie to be torn in pieces." The conservative Randolph observed that the queen was "seized with love in fervanter passions than is comely for any mean personage."[2] He felt she had no shame, no honor, no care for her subjects. His hatred toward Darnley and the Lennox-Stuarts was great. Darnley's pride was intolerable, unbearable. No one was allowed to disagree with the nineteen-year-old. "Passions and furies he will sometimes be in are strange to believe." Randolph observed Darnley ranging from "uncontrollable passion to maudlin repentance." Already he seemed to be forgetting his duty to Mary. Apparently, too, Darnley had begun to drink excessively.

MUCH OF SCOTLAND WAS ANGRY and blamed Elizabeth for sending Darnley. Her brother James, who had been an excellent advisor to Mary during her reign, was very much opposed to the match, and very much out of favor with Darnley. When he told Mary that he opposed the marriage, she insulted her brother by accusing him of wanting the crown for himself. James left the court in April furious.

Her great champion Throckmorton felt helpless in the face of Mary's commitment to Darnley, and concluded to Elizabeth that Mary had "been so captivated, either by love or cunning (or rather, to say truly, by boasting or folly) that she is not able to keep promise with herself, and therefore not most able to keep promise with your majesty in these matters."

Elizabeth sent word that she disapproved, that marrying Darnley would "seriously endanger Anglo-Scottish friendship," which astonished Mary, who had believed that Elizabeth would be pleased she had chosen an Englishman. Darnley, however, being Catholic and in succession to her throne, appeared more threatening than a foreign prince to Elizabeth. She commanded Darnley and his father to return to England—an order that they ignored. She then sent Darnley's mother, Lady Lennox, to the tower for treason, which did nothing to get the two most important men in the extremely ambitious lady's life home. Mary, already weary of playing mouse to Elizabeth, could not imagine the English queen would be satisfied by any gesture on her part.

Mary discounted the loss of Elizabeth saying she had the approval of the "greatest Princes in Christendom"; she was able to get the approval from her French relations and King Philip of Spain. The king of Spain's blessings, however, came at a price. He insisted that Mary follow his dictates in all things "without swerving a hair's breadth from them": which meant the hideous methods of religious enslavement, characteristic of Spanish Catholicism, were to be employed in crushing her own subjects, much like with Mary Tudor's regime. England and Scotland would be a blood bath. Mary's original policy of religious liberty would no longer prevail. Her French interests would suffer horribly. Blinded by love, she suddenly did not see the "treachery and wickedness of her aims." If she had known to just wait, she would have seen her folly before it was too late.

The only true supporter of the marriage was the Italian David Riccio, Mary's new secretary handling her French correspondence and musician to her court, who was "thick as thieves with Darnley." As all close to her who objected fell out of favor, Mary began to rely more and more on David Riccio.

About Darnley, "it was foreseen that the young fool and proud tyrant would fare badly in a country where the blow of a dagger was the answer to a peevish word." Perhaps it was only because he was young and had won their queen's heart, that so many of the nobles of kindred arrogance and violence condemned him. But within two years, Riccio and Darnley would be murdered, and Mary would marry her husband's murderer.

On July 22, 1565, the banns were published in the Canongate Kirk, St. Giles. The queen had made Darnley the Duke of Albany the day before. On the 28th of July at 9 p.m., "Three heralds stood at the Market Cross of Edinburgh and with a flourish of trumpets announced that the queen had resolved to wed . . . and that Prince Henry, Duke of Albany, would be named King of this our kingdom." Without Parliament's consent, the queen's declaration was illegal. "But Mary refused her bridegroom nothing his pride did not covet."

On Sunday morning, July 29, before six in the morning, Mary, dressed in mourning robes and a wide widow's hood, walked radiantly down the aisle of the chapel royal of Holyrood Palace, accompanied by Darnley's father, Lennox, and the earl of Argyll, one of the leading Protestant lords. Seven persons in all were present. It had been seven years since her sumptuous wedding in Paris. Mary was left alone at the altar as Lennox walked back down the aisle to then escort his son, now King Henry of Scotland, who was dressed in splendid attire with glittering gems. Banns were proclaimed for the third time. As they pledged their troth, valuable rings were exchanged. Three rings were placed on Mary's finger, the middle one a beautiful diamond. After prayers and blessings were said, the groom kissed the bride on the lips and left her to hear their nuptial Mass alone.

The court was deathly still all day. After Mass the queen had found her groom awaiting her in her own bedchamber. She presented herself as blushing and shy about removing her mourning clothes, more for manner's sake than grief of heart according to Randolph. Ritualistically, she allowed all in the room to each take one pin from her hair. Then, with the help of her handmaidens, she changed into her bridal finery, finally ending her state of mourning for her first husband. She did not go straight to bed with her new groom, though, in order to signify that she did not marry for lust, although that was the only excuse anyone could come up with to make sense of Mary's choice. During the afternoon, the couple

Anonymous, 16th c.
Double portrait of
Mary and Lord
Darnley.
(National Trust/Art
Resource, NY)

Fattori, Giovanni (1825-1908). Mary Stuart at the Battle
of Carberry Hill, 1567.
(Art Resource, NY)

walked through the town in disguise until returning for the evening's magnificent celebration of their nuptials. Trumpets sounded, largess cried and money was thrown about to all. There was dancing, and then a respite until dinner when the festivities began all over again.

Finally the couple went to their wedding bed. Naturally there was wide speculation about whether this was their first night together. Randolph attributed any rumors stating they had already consummated their romance to the malice of her enemies. Being so close to the queen, Randolph felt he could say with assurance that the "likelihoods are so great to the contrary." Many days of celebration and masques followed the wedding. Knox complained, "During the space of three or four days, there was nothing but balling, and dancing and banqueting."

Mary had sent for dispensation from the pope, which was needed because she and Darnley were such near relations. Assuming it was coming, she rushed her wedding before it arrived; most likely their passions could not wait much longer. She misjudged, however, and dispensation was not granted until after the wedding had taken place, which meant in effect their marriage was invalid, a fact that was never made public.

The marriage ended Mary Stuart's political capital, while the queen of England continued to play her possible suitors like a finely-tuned fiddle, wooing one then turning around and dropping that one for another to gain whatever pressing advantage at the time. With Mary's marriage to the Catholic, Darnley, and Philip II's conditional approval, all feared Spain. But Mary insisted she would never take away their religious freedom, and made no moves in that direction.

After her marriage, Mary no longer spoke with "bated breath and whispering humbleness." One observer noted: "I find her marvelously stout and such as one I could not have believed." Mary was very much in command now. She even dropped her gentle deference to her "good sister" in England in the face of Elizabeth's lack of support. If Elizabeth thought the marriage made Mary vulnerable, she seriously underestimated her younger cousin's fearlessness and determination.

The only person to have her under his thumb now was her husband, and she handed her rule over to him while the honeymoon lasted. Even though, in her best judgment, she felt they should wait until Darnley turned twenty-one to make him officially king, Darnley insisted they not wait a day, and she relented, knowing full well that they would both be less respected. The day after their wedding, the heralds announced once more the fact that Darnley was now king, and Mary further proclaimed that from then on all official documents and proclamations would carry both their signatures. An ominous silence fell among the nobles. None proclaimed him king, this "raw-boned lad of nineteen." He was "foolish, ignorant, ill-conditioned, vicious, without a single manly quality" to all but Mary. Only his doting father declared in a proud and booming voice that echoed through the deadly silent hall, "God save his Grace!"

OVER THE SUMMER MONTHS and into the fall, all who were stunned by Mary's irrational behavior in marrying Darnley were now enormously impressed by her brilliant ability to be in command. Rather than attributing this sudden change in personality, from the meek and obedient young maiden who joyfully pleased everyone to a woman fully in her own power, to her husband, it must be realized this talented and passionate, intelligent, courageous and educated young woman had been on hold—at least in her own mind—waiting to know her own fate through the man she would marry. A great deal of energy had been tied up as she waited, and now this energy was released and available to be of service to herself and her country. In her hardness after years of learning how to survive, Elizabeth had learned to play everyone around her, and was always in charge of her own life. Mary, on the other hand, had felt herself to be all the pieces on the chessboard at different times, but never the one to move them.

Rather than staying by Mary's side to help her come to her senses after the bloom of the honeymoon, her brother James openly revolted against her and mortal hatred developed between the two. Drumming up support for his cause, he fanned fears that Mary was planning now to reinstate Catholicism, despite all evidence to the contrary. She married a man who could hardly be called a devout Catholic. Several times, Darnley listened to Knox preach at St. Giles Church, and he had avoided attending his own nuptial Mass, which Mary seemed to easily forgive, never desiring to impose her beliefs on another. Her deep devotion to the Mass and the strength it gave her were essential to her, and she could not begin anything, much less a marriage, without the healing power of the ritual. That her husband did not share her devotion did not diminish hers. That her country made other choices was acceptable to her.

However, after his marriage, Darnley had sat uncomfortably on the specially prepared throne as he listened to Knox preach: "I will give children to be their princes, and babes shall rule over them." Knox harangued the young king, pontificating that God had punished Ahab because he did not correct his idolatrous wife, Jezebel, but in these degenerate times, Ahab joined Jezebel in her idolatry. Darnley flew out of the church in a rage and went hawking. Mary demanded Knox come before her that very evening. Given that he had insulted the king (who was not present during the reprimand) he must not preach while the sovereigns were in the capital. Knox replied he was speaking the word of God.

Mary had the power to unilaterally silence the self-appointed, slanderous and pompous mouthpiece, but she would not out of deep personal respect for his freedom of speech and religion. With only ancient echoes of Henry Wallace, Robert the Bruce and the archaic Druids to support her, Mary Stuart, queen of Scots was actually the first ruler to attempt to, by proclamation and diplomacy, implement the doctrine of the rights of the individual to freedom of personal expression, and endeavor to facilitate the peaceful worship of two different religions within one country. Her struggles were the seed of a new idea, a democracy, which would find, more than a century later, fertile soil in a new country thousands of miles away. Few would remember the forerunner for such a radical idea.

Where she herself proclaimed it for Protestants, Knox was fearful of allowing Catholics to worship freely, feeling that all his zealous efforts would be undone. Unfortunately for her Catholic subjects, who most likely would have been tolerant of the Protestants, the new pope, Pius V definitely had a different agenda. He wrote to Mary:

> Most dear daughter—We have heard with the utmost joy that you and his Highness, your husband, have lately given brilliant proof of your zeal by restoring the due worship of God throughout your whole realm. Truly, dearest daughter, you understand the duties of devout kings and queens . . .

He further encouraged her to weed out completely "the thorns and tares of heretical depravity . . ."

Her marriage so shook the country at first, especially with her brother's rebellion and the fears of her Catholic background, that Mary had all she could handle to dissipate their distrust. "In this hour of danger, she showed herself to be a worthy daughter of her race."[3] The root of her brother's defection was his feudal hatred of the Catholic Lennox-Stuarts, and his open rebellion had to be answered. She commanded his presence to explain himself and offered safe-conduct, but he refused.

Always bold in a crisis, the queen of Scots rode out of Edinburgh toward the west of Scotland "at the head of her troops, in high spirits, with a pistol at her saddle bow and swearing revenge on her enemies," who had dared disobey their sovereign. Only one woman accompanied her. Her high-spirited appeal drew to her an army of seven thousand men. Mary was the "best man in Scotland" at this point. She stayed in the saddle through the foulest weather, on hazardous paths, for twenty miles a day. Accompanying his wife, trussed in his finery, Darnley was a "poor fribble" in comparison with his regal wife. Even Knox had to praise her for the leadership of her troops: "Albeit the most part waxed weary, yet the queen's courage increased man-like, so much that she was ever with the foremost."

During her absence, her brother and his rebellious nobles entered Edinburgh but there was no support there for their coup from either Protestants or Catholics. The people loved their beautiful queen unequivocally and, after four years of her rule, trusted her. The queen of Scots had the common touch to reach their hearts that the nobles of her kingdom entirely lacked.

Accompanying her on her pursuit of the renegade nobles was James Bothwell, who had hurried from France to his queen's side upon her request and pardon of his crimes against her. Bothwell was a sworn enemy of her brother and suited her purposes perfectly. He was restored to his office of lieutenant of the middle marshes and quickly appointed to the Privy Council, despite his nasty comments at his ordered departure from Scotland, that Mary was "the cardinal's whore, and that she and Elizabeth between them did not add up to one honest woman." His forceful and purposeful nature served his queen well and he took a leadership position at once.

In October, run out of Scotland, James appealed to Elizabeth, who he thought would naturally desire to assist Protestantism against his papist sister. Instead, he was humiliated and rejected, receiving a slap on the wrist for rebelling against his sister, and decided to retreat for a while.

Mary spent her honeymoon defending her choice of a husband. All were expected to treat him royally and obey him as king. Her feelings were still tender and loyal toward her husband, perhaps even maternal given he was four years younger and they fell in love while he was on his sickbed. Perhaps she tolerated some of his behavior because she also looked at him in some ways as if he were a child. Her feelings for Francois, too, had, most likely been more maternal than anything else. On her arrival in Scotland, despite her young years, she looked upon her subjects with motherly affection. More than the carnal reasons attributed by all for her sudden marriage to Darnley, he may have also evoked in her strong maternal feelings. She had never known her father, and, despite all the years they spent apart, the love she felt from her mother was the most unconditional and warm she would ever know.

Until Darnley was awarded the crown matrimonial he was not considered his wife's equal, and would not inherit the crown in case of her death. Her signature appeared on the left, the more important position, on all documents. At times, Darnley would peevishly try to assert himself by signing his name larger than the queen's. The hand of his ambitious father was obvious at those times, since Darnley could not have cared less about governing a country, preferring hunting and hawking and the constant pursuit of pleasure. Most nights he spent getting drunk. Darnley's father, Lennox, though, wanted the crown for his family. If Darnley did get his back up, it was more that he was aware of being perceived as weaker than his wife. He should be in command. That she was, he thought, was shameful. If such opinions weren't also being voiced to him by others, he may not have cared. On top of everything, Elizabeth refused to accept any document with Darnley's signature, as she did not recognize him as king in any capacity, but only as her subject and an offender to her crown.

MARY STUART'S MARRIAGE was a fatal sacrifice. In no way was her husband a source of strength, either politically or as a husband. It did not take Mary long to realize her husband was all show and could be counted on for nothing, "a painted lath instead of a trusty blade."

If Mary had been more like Elizabeth and Catherine de' Medici and enjoyed conspiracy, she would have enthusiastically joined in the game of playing off her nobles, with their self-aggrandizing agendas, and found protection for herself. But her nature was too forthright and candid to enjoy intrigue. Her passionate temperment preferred action, commitment and simplicity, and had little patience for intrigue. For this reason, and not just because they did not support her husband, Mary began to look outside the tangled web of noble families for her advisors. In order to rule on her own terms, she knew she needed to break the stranglehold of the overbearing nobility, so used to manipulating each other and their sovereign. She needed to break free of Elizabeth's attempts at domination, and so she threw off the tutelage of Maitland and her brother.

Of her new advisors, all outside the circle of the self-interested nobility, the Italian David Riccio became the most prominent. Riccio first arrived in Scotland with the Savoyard ambassador in 1561. All remarked he was an ugly little man, but a jolly fellow and an excellent musician with a fine bass voice. He filled out Mary's quartet of singers. Able to converse with her about parts of the world she had never seen, and relate to the French court she knew, he was a great companion, especially during those times when she was starved for the refinements missing in the Scottish court. At first he helped her with her private papers and then he was promoted to private secretary. She trusted him. He did not appear to have any agendas with her, other than enjoying his own love of the finer things of life. And he was loyal, a quality she valued more than any other in anyone close to her.

As she came to rely more and more on Riccio's natural abilities and total devotion, he, not surprisingly, became detestable to the nobles. After all, they hated each other, but at least they knew with whom they were playing their deadly games. David Riccio, of an aristocratic Italian family whose fortunes had turned for the worse, was thought of as "the brain of the queen's clique and a low-born foreigner." No one approved and the situation was becoming dangerous. The nobles were not going to remain out of the center of power for long. Her enemies began to drop black hints.

Mary was criticized as being an entirely different woman from the one in happier days when she listened to worthy counsel and "her praise ran through all nations." Randolph swore, "A more willful woman, and one more wedded unto her own opinion, without order or reason or discretion, I never did know or hear of." Mary wasn't arrogant though. She had asked Sir James Melville to watch over her conduct and to warn her if she was ever to "forget herself by unseemly gesture or behavior," or do anything that might make her unpopular with her subjects. Melville did warn her that her public familiarity with Riccio was outraging many, and Mary pulled back some.

In the fall, when she knew she was pregnant, she naturally became aware at a deeper level of her extreme vulnerability, surrounded by men she must count on, none of whom she could trust, and with a husband who could be counted on for little if anything. Riccio became more and more important to her. As the months passed and the new year began, treachery beyond anything the unsuspecting queen could imagine was developing.

As Mary Stuart's personal power grew, the rift between husband and wife became the weapon the scheming nobles used to undermine her. At a public entertainment in Edinburgh, there was a nasty scene between Mary and Darnley. Mary left in tears after trying unsuccessfully to restrain her husband from drinking too much. Not a fool, she withdrew her promise of the crown matrimonial, now knowing how disruptive his instability could be for the country and seeing no hope of a sudden change of character. His vanity and ambitions thwarted, Darnley got even by throwing a series of debauched parties. Rumors flew of affairs with ladies of the court. After learning of an incident so unspeakably disgraceful, Mary ceased sharing a bed with her husband.

The nobles despicably played with Darnley's weaknesses. Riccio became the scapegoat, and the nobles were easily able to convince Darnley his wife was the short, unappealing Italian's mistress. "Villain Davey" had done him "the most dishonour that can be to any man." Darnley was an easy dupe. Whether they continued down the road of that trail of thought to further inflame him, or Darnley's own jealous mind went straight to the idea, he began to wonder if the baby his wife was carrying was really Riccio's. It would not take great powers of observation to know that this was impossible, but Darnley was convinced and rumors spread, further embarrassing the king into some kind of action.

Having wooed him with his own jealous rage, they captured him for their side by convincing him he rightfully should be king and rule in place of his wife. If she were to die, and also the baby, he would be the natural successor against the nearest claimants, the Hamilton family. The king thus convinced, Mary's brother James and his supporters would have a puppet on the throne and return themselves to the seat of power, if they could survive the peril of the king's family, the Lennox-Stuarts's drive for full power. In Scotland, "men suffered from few inhibitions when it came to the liquidation of an unpopular public figure."[4]

Elizabeth I involved herself in the controversy by requesting that Mary pardon her brother and not banish Randolph, who had begun to be the number-one perpetrator of the rumor mill. She gave James one thousand pounds in aid. Mary did not consent, and further requested that Parliament draw up a bill of attainder against James; the date of its issuance was to be March 12. Somehow, Mary either did not know of the conspiracy against her or did not believe it. As an advisor, Riccio's own arrogance blinded him to the dangers near at hand. Damiot the astrologer warned him, "Beware the bastard!" Riccio dismissed the Scots as all boasting, but little threat. Mary's response was much the same: "Our countrymen are well-wordy."

Exactly one year had passed since Darnley first arrived on Scottish soil. Randolph wrote to Dudley, earl of Leicester: "I know for certain that this Queen repenteth her marriage, that she hateth her husband and all his kin. I know there are practices in hand contrived between father and son to come by the crown against her will. I know if that take effect which is intended, David, with the consent of the King shall have his throat cut within these ten days. Many things grievouser and worse than these are brought to my ears, yea, of things intended against her own person."

If the nobles had qualms, Darnley's father had none about murdering his daughter-in-law and first grandchild to secure the throne for himself.

11

The Hale Birlin' World

Dinna think it wis lichtsomely or in love
that I lay me doon wi' ye, in the daurk.
Naw, it wis in despair.
Oh and wi' a kinna black joy I reachit oot for you
to cover me and smother me and for yin moment,
snuff oot the hale birlin' world in stillness.

—*Liz Lochead*

ON THE TERRIBLE EVENING of Saturday, March 9, in her tiny supper room, within the turret at the northwest corner of Holyrood Palace that held her suite of four rooms, Mary hosted an intimate dinner party. The twelve by twelve-foot supper room was draped in crimson and green. Nearby was the narrow stairwell that led to the king's apartments below. As her pregnancy advanced, now six months along, Mary was less inclined to go out at night to Edinburgh, preferring quieter entertainment at home. This night she invited her half-brother Lord Robert Stewart, her half-sister and confidante Jean, countess of Argyll, Arthur Erskine her horseman and Anthony Standen her page. Davey Riccio was also there, either to provide music or to play cards later as he often did with the queen, sometimes until two in the morning, much to the resentment of the king. Meat was served, despite it being Lent, as the queen's condition permitted it.

Out of nowhere it seemed, because he had been so quiet, the

king appeared at the top of the privy staircase. Always welcomed but rarely seen, as his pleasures were usually partaken in the streets of Edinburgh, he took all by surprise. But more startling was the sudden appearance of the sinister Patrick Lord Ruthven, not only because he was never invited, but also because it had been known that the reputed warlock had been on his deathbed. When the little company noticed Ruthven was wearing armor under his robes, they all thought he must have been delusional from fever, imagining himself being pursued by some enemy.

But then a chill filled the room as Ruthven spoke directly to the queen. "Let it please your Majesty, that yonder man David come forth of your privy-chamber where he hath been overlong." Indignant, the queen responded that David had been invited, and then turned toward her husband when it dawned on her who the instigator was. As if reading a warrant, Ruthven denounced Mary's relations with Riccio. All the while, Riccio inched his way backward toward the window. When Ruthven lunged toward him with his dagger, Mary's little party struggled to hold him back. Hanging halfway out the window, Riccio drew his own dagger. As Ruthven then cried out against them, "Lay not hands on me, for I will not be handled," his gang of five thugs, including George Douglas, stormed into the room wielding daggers and pistols. The board fell from the wall along with the meat and candles. One candle was saved by Lady Argyll just before it fell to the floor and was extinguished. Valiantly, she held the candle up against the darkened and violence-filled room, illuminated now solely by the embers in the fireplace and her one candle.

David Riccio clung desperately to the queen's skirts, feeling safer by her, never imagining the assassins were hopeful for the worst for his queen as well. As his fingers were pried loose from her skirts, Riccio was dragged, screaming piteously for Mary to save him, into the adjoining room and through the presence chamber to the head of the stairs. The first wound to the Italian was delivered by George Douglas, bastard brother of Lord Morton, fulfilling the astrologer's prophecy, "Beware the bastard!" Douglas used Darnley's own dagger to deepen the king's involvement in the horrendous murder. The tiny tortured body sustained a brutal fifty-three-plus knife wounds as they all fell on him, before throwing his bloody corpse down the winding stairwell.

All the while, a pistol was held to the queen's belly. Although she could not see the brutality, she could hear every bit of it. The horror of listening to the sickening blows of so many knife stabs; the extreme brutality—these were calculated to cause the queen to miscarry, which meant certain death in the sixteenth century. If Riccio had been the only target, he could have been done away with in a much easier fashion apart from the queen.

While the assassins took off to deal with Riccio's body, Mary was left alone with Darnley. Not for a moment intimidated by the events, Mary turned in fury at her husband. When Ruthven returned, he was not spared. As Ruthven continued to preach to her about her improprieties against her husband, she scorned him saying she had "that within in her belly, which would one day be revenged upon him." As he sipped his wine trying to recuperate, Ruthven hardly feared the fruit of her womb, as he believed a miscarriage to be imminent. As it would turn out, Mary prophesied true. Her child would put to death Ruthven's son and grandson in two different conspiracies: the son in eighteen years, and the grandson in thirty-four.

The alarm bell of the city sounded. Townsfolk gathered, drawn by the cries of terror and all the commotion. Instinctively Mary moved toward the window to reassure them, but was violently restrained and threatened. Darnley, now bloated with his victory and pumped up by Ruthven, asserted his sovereignty over his queen, and went to the window himself as their king to calm them.

Finally, the men departed, leaving Mary alone with no medical care. When the messenger she sent to inquire about Riccio returned with the confirmation that he was indeed dead, she wept for a moment then dried her tears, pulled herself together, and declared, "No more tears—I will think upon revenge."

This was the night that would reveal the greatness of Mary Stuart's extraordinary spirit. The conspirators against her throne had triumphed, and one of the conspirators was her husband. In effect, she was their prisoner. At best she would be kept alive until the birth of her child, who would then become their pawn. She also must have known that her husband had also wanted her and their baby dead. The enormous effort it took to overcome her revulsion toward her husband and do what she did next is almost impossible to imagine. Although her actions only forestalled her own seemingly inevitable tragedy, she was able to keep Scotland on its course toward eventual peace, and keep alive her son who would become a great king of both Scotland and England. The only other leadership left for the country, without Mary and her son, was the weak and corruptible Darnley and the unscrupulous nobles, who would have lead the country in a very different direction.

SOME GOODNESS OR CONSCIENCE must have lurked inside the heart of Darnley, unless he was just too cowardly to face the consequences of his actions. He returned the next morning, rather hysterical, to the queen's apartments. Invoking his favorite endearment, "Ah, my Mary," he pleaded with his wife to forgive him his incomprehensible betrayal. Drawing on formidable courage, resolution and self control, Mary received him calmly, without reproach, and during the course of the day managed to convince him he was ultimately in as much peril as she, and they needed to join forces or both would be dead. To get her spineless husband to betray his betrayers as he had betrayed her and their unborn child was her only hope.

Part of Mary's plan was to also woo the conspirators into complacency by pardoning them their hideous crimes. On Monday, using all her charms to persuade them of her sincerity, she drank a toast, although she could not make herself drink to Ruthven. As she had granted all their requests, she asked Maitland to remove the guards.

What she did not understand was that her brother James had been the foremost instigator of the assassination plot. So, when he returned to Edinburgh on Monday, she threw herself into his arms in relief at seeing him—the younger sister who had for most of her life been protected by her older brother. If only he had been there, she told him, "he would not have suffered her to be so uncourteously handled." Instead of comfort Mary received a condescending lecture from James on clemency, despite the fact she had pardoned everyone. Indignant, Mary responded that, "Ever since her earliest youth, her nobility and others of her people had given her frequent opportunities of practicing that virtue and becoming familiar with it."

To further throw the conspirators off, Mary suddenly feigned illness and withdrew to her rooms with the midwife her enemies provided. Given the horrible ordeal Mary had just been through, the midwife had no problem declaring to her evil employers that the queen was indeed in grave danger, and thus she quite nicely played her part in Mary's plan. Monday evening, disconcerted by the violence of their henchmen and now worried about Queen Elizabeth's reaction, James and Maitland called off the "Douglas cutthroats," and retired to have dinner and rethink their plans. Unwisely, they left Darnley behind.

Meanwhile, Mary sent for John Stewart of Traquair, captain of the Royal Guard, Arthur Erskine her Master of the Horse and her page Anthony Standen. Appealing to their gallantry in the name of her unborn child, the future ruler of Scotland, Mary asked them to help her make her escape that very evening.

Just after midnight, Mary and Darnley made their escape using the same privy stairs that had been the access for her near destruction. Riccio's mutilated body had lain at the bottom only two nights before. Without Darnley, Mary never would have had passage through his rooms, the only avenue of escape for her. Through the kitchen and past her French servants who would never betray her, they found their way outside the walls of the Holyrood. Nearby was the royal chapel of the palace, and Riccio's freshly dug grave. As they slipped by the grim reminder of his cowardice, Darnley pointed out the grave to his wife, and perhaps indicating the beginnings of a developing conscience, told her, "In him I have lost a good and faithful servant. I have been miserably cheated."

Under cover of the black night, Mary mounted Erskine's horse behind him. Darnley, growing more and more fearful of the men he just betrayed, urged them all to keep up an intense pace, despite the queen's vulnerable condition. Mary pleaded with Darnley to go slower, but in his panic, Darnley flew into a rage and declared it did not matter if the baby died; they would have more. The grueling twenty-mile ride to Dunbar Castle on the Lothian Coast took five hours. They did not stop once. Despite her ordeal, the queen sent for eggs to cook breakfast herself for everyone after their arrival.

Seeking by any means to keep peace in her country, Mary took immediate and bold action, and once again emerged victorious against her enemies. First she drove a wedge between the conspirators by reneging on her promises of pardon, and only forgiving her brother, though by now Darnley must have told her of James' major role in the conspiracy against her. She then set about telling the world of the recent events.

In her letter to Elizabeth, Mary apologized for not writing in her own hand, explaining, "of truth we are so tired and evil at ease, what through riding of twenty miles in five hours of the night, as with the frequent sickness and evil disposition by the occasion of our child," it proved too difficult. Queen Elizabeth was the most upset of the European rulers, and took to wearing a miniature likeness of the queen of Scots, hung by a gold chain from her waist. Elizabeth told the Spanish ambassador to her court that had she been in Mary's place, she would have "seized her treacherous husband's dagger and stabbed him with it." There is no doubt she would have.

Two other targets of the conspirators, Bothwell and Huntley, had managed to escape assassination the night of Riccio's brutal murder by climbing out a window overlooking the lion pit. Along with Lords Atholl, Fleming and Seton, they rushed to Mary's aid at Dunbar Castle. For his loyalty, Bothwell was given the rights to Dunbar Castle, which would play an important role in Mary's near future.

ONLY NINE DAYS had passed, when on March 18, Mary returned triumphantly to Edinburgh at the head of an army of 8,000 men commanded by the earl of Bothwell, her husband the king now skulking along like a shamefaced knave. Darnley had been publicly proclaimed innocent, even though his fellow conspirators sent Mary the bond Darnley had signed as proof against him. Although proclaimed innocent, he was now given the cold shoulder by Mary and universally despised. All the defectors, plus a few like Knox who lent their moral support to the plan, had left town the day before. Her brother, finally pardoned as Elizabeth and others had urged when she married Darnley, was able to remain.

Immediately upon her return, Mary arranged for a proper Catholic burial for her cherished servant. Riccio's eighteen-year-old brother was given his brother's former position. She established a new Privy Council, reconciling long-standing feuds among the nobles now loyal to her. Her brother, James, and Lords Glencairn and Argyll now became her advisors alongside their old enemies Bothwell, Huntley and Atholl. Just as Throckmorton had observed at the beginning of her reign of Scotland, when reflecting on the effect of her rule on England, should that ever come to pass, "This benefit all should have from her— that she would answer with mind and intent to win all hearts, being void of partialities, affectionate to no faction, free from inveterate malice and desire to revenge displeasures and things past." Unfortunately, such noble qualities did little to protect her from the men of such an opposite nature that surrounded her. Only Bothwell of the nobles was able to come close to mirroring her courage, strength and sophistication.

As she began to nest in earnest, to prepare herself and the country for the birth of her child and heir to the Scottish throne, Mary again used all her forces of discretion, conciliation and prudent state craft to ensure a peaceful kingdom for her babe. This meant maintaining her marriage with Darnley, even though she grew to abhor him more and more every day, as he continued his scandalous habits, and as the truth of his betrayal sunk in deeper after the crises was over. She could not risk the chance of her child being considered illegitimate and losing the throne, even though a divorce would have been a humane solution for her.

Instead of returning to Holyrood, the better-protected Edinburgh Castle became her new residence. As she, in anticipating childbirth in the sixteenth century, was "in peril and danger of her life," she made a will. Everything was to go to her child upon her death. But, if they both died, a major portion of her riches were to go to Scotland, although there was plenty left over to bequeath to all her relations, both French and Scottish, and her servants who were always also loyal friends.

Rooms in the southeast corner of the old palace, overlooking the town, were taken over as the queen's lying-in chamber, which she entered on the third of June, two weeks before her expected delivery date. Her bed was elegantly draped with blue velvet and blue taffeta, and great amounts of cloth from Holland decorated the baby's cradle. The actual birthing room was tiny. The midwife was given a black velvet dress to wear during the birth. After a false alarm on June 15, a long and painful labor began three days later. In her pain, Mary screamed out her regrets at ever having married. Efforts were made to cast a spell by witchcraft and place Mary's suffering onto a willing subject, Lady Reres, but of course to no avail.

Finally, around ten or eleven on the morning of June 19, 1566, the infant prince, called James, was born healthy and strong. A filmy caul stretched over his face, as if to eerily symbolize that in only months, his mother would never again look on the face of her son. The difficult labor cost Mary dearly. Five days after, she was only able to speak faintly and she had developed a hollow cough. Her health would never be the same.

The city of Edinburgh rejoiced. Five hundred bonfires were lit in celebration. The view from the birthing rooms was stirring. All the artillery of the castle was fired, and St. Giles church was overflowing with grateful citizens. There was hope of one of theirs ruling over England some day. When Sir James Melville reported the birth of the new prince of Scotland to Queen Elizabeth, her outcry was bitter. "The Queen of Scots was lighter of a fair son, while I am but a barren stock."

As if finally able after his birth to ensure no repercussions to her child by an estrangement, Mary angrily announced to her husband, "I have forgiven, but never will forget! What if Fawdon's pistol had shot, what would become of him and me both? Or what estate would you have been in? God only knows, but we may suspect." To end any rumors of another being the father of her child—Darnley had been told and may have still believed—and to erase any possible stigma of illegitimacy, Mary displayed their son to Darnley in public, announcing: "My Lord, God has given you and me a son, begotten by none but you." As she uncovered their son's face, she continued, "Here I protest to God as I shall answer to him at the great day of Judgment, that this is your son and no other man's son. I am desirous that all here, with ladies and others bear witness." It had to have been with a great deal of grief that she added, "For he is so much your own son, that I fear it will be the worse for him hereafter." She no longer had any need to pretend.

MARY WAS A DEVOTED MOTHER in the short time she had with her child. She cared for him personally and he slept in her own room, most times watching over him herself during the night. When the infant James was just a few days old, Mary sent for Anthony Standen, who had heroically helped her escape. She honored him by making him a knight. Pointing to the heir to the Scottish throne, peacefully sleeping in his cradle, Mary said, "For that you saved his life . . ." As if an angel had spoken to her, she turned to a young English soldier and declared: "This is the son who shall unite the two kingdoms of England and Scotland." The tiny prince would indeed fulfill his mother's prophecy, but at great cost. His father would be murdered, some would believe under the direction of his own mother, within eight months of his birth. Two months later, his mother would be forced to surrender to her enemies, and he would never see her again. He would be crowned king, after his mother's coerced abdication.

Over the summer, the queen of Scots grew ever more vulnerable, even as she grew stronger as a ruler. She now also had her son to protect. Still searching for advisors she could trust, after Riccio's assassination and the betrayal of her husband and brother, Mary began to quite naturally lean toward someone who understood the nobles and could play their game—but better—and whom she could still trust to be loyal to her. A sensitive, intelligent, card-playing Italian musician was obviously not protection enough.

Bothwell began to win her trust, and as his esteem increased, so did his enemies, who began to hate him as much as they had hated

Riccio. Although known as a ladies man, Bothwell, who had recently married into the important Huntley family, was never linked romantically or sexually with Mary Stuart until after the death of Darnley, when in "hindsight" her enemies spread rumors of their secret liaisons. Mary had barely enough physical energy after the birth of her son to deal with her very pressing problems of state and the deterioration of her marriage, let alone begin a passionate affair. But clearly she was leaning on him more for advice and, more importantly, protection.

Her marital difficulties could no longer be hidden. Eruptions in public became common. Extraordinarily jealous, now even of her women friends, Darnley's touchiest issue was feeling humiliated by his wife, although he was not about to change his behavior toward her. He took everything personally, and never hesitated to humiliate Mary. When once she declined to go hunting, pleading that she may be pregnant again, he again, like during their escape after Riccio's death, demanded she do what he wished saying they can have another. When their host, Traquair, rebuked him, Darnley snarled back, "What! Ought not we to work a mare well when she is in foal?" The spat revealed that Mary and Darnley did have intimate relations after the birth of their son, which was actually a dangerous situation for the queen. Another pregnancy would tie her longer to him, and it was soon to become obvious that he suffered from syphilis.

In late summer, Prince James, now two months old, was moved to Stirling Castle, the traditional nursery for tiny royalty. Giving over to the Erskines, as hereditary governors, the fostering of her son, Mary was following a practice in place among the nobility for centuries. A stamp of aristocracy, the custom of fostering later began to be followed by those of the aspiring social classes. Her love for her tiny son was apparent. If she could not be with him every moment, she made sure that he was surrounded by all the best that she could possibly provide. Her succor extended to her son's wet nurse, Lady Reres. Nothing was to be spared her comfort.

It is difficult to imagine, given Mary's naturally maternal nature and her love of children, that being apart from her baby did not cause some level of deep distress for her. In the pleasure of providing for his needs during the last of the warm summer days, Mary had no idea that her son would be living out a motherless boyhood at Stirling. From his stern and scholarly taskmaster, George Buchanan, her son would be taught Latin before he could speak Scots, and would be disciplined by watching a whipping boy vicariously receive his punishment. When he learned to write, he would refer to his imprisoned mother as "That renowned queen, my mother." Brought up by her enemies, he would be raised Protestant, and to believe she was responsible for his father's murder.

While she directed the decorating and the caretakers in his new little nest, Mary also began planning her son's christening. Looking to more closely bind her cousin to her new little nephew and ensure her interest in making him the successor to her throne, Elizabeth was asked to be godmother. The queen of England accepted, although she would be unable to attend the December ceremony. Instead she sent as a gift a solid gold baptismal font.

On October 16, Mary and a few of her nobles rode fifty miles in one day to visit Bothwell, believed to be on his deathbed after being injured during a border skirmish. This ride, although a difficult one, was not a hardship for the queen, so used to long rides in the saddle. Hermitage Castle was too close to the English border to safely house the queen overnight. But she needed to see her trusted advisor. And so the long journey that became part of Queen Mary's legend was made. For romantics and for Mary's enemies, this trip was believed to be the beginning of, if not an indication of, an already long-standing passionate relationship for Mary with Bothwell, despite the fact that her party could have stayed only a few hours.

Perhaps the intensity of her illness after returning from visiting Bothwell contributed to the drama of the journey. The queen nearly lost her life, and for a half hour at one point, everyone thought she had died. Always, emotional stress would finally take its toll on Mary's health, until she could rise again as if from the ashes. Mary believed it was her deep grief and sorrow over the breakdown of her marriage that had caused her sudden, life-threatening illness. She was well aware of Darnley's continued plots against her. Maitland, who had been recently reinstated into Mary's good graces, wrote to her ambassador to France, "For she honored him greatly, despite contrary advice, and in return, the king is ungrateful . . . He misuses himself so far towards her that it breaks her heart to think he is her husband." Mary desperately wished be free of Darnley, but she saw no way out.

Facing death once more, Mary again revealed her real interests. Making sure her son succeeded her and was protected from a coup by his father was her primary concern. She needed promises that the young prince would have no evil company around him growing up. His father had blamed his own problems to corruption he had experienced through his companions. Again, she declared publicly that Darnley's behavior was the cause of her illness. She also asked that after her death, her Catholic subjects be treated with the same tolerance that she had treated her Protestant subjects.

By the end of November, Mary had survived, but she was in a deep depression and often said, "I could wish to be dead." Living with the constant threat of conspiracy by Darnley was wearing her out. If there were another way to look at the situation, none was presented to her. The nobles, especially Mary's brother James, equally despised Darnley. Mary's good-hearted and gay nature could not sustain such negativity as surrounded her. Maitland, Bothwell, her brother and others began to ask her to leave it to them when she asked for protection after a divorce. Their request was for a pardon of the lords involved in Riccio's murder, which she granted. She told them she had two requests: first, that nothing jeopardize her son or his succession; and, second, that nothing is done against her honor. A bond was drawn up and signed among the nobles to rid the country of the "young fool and proud tyrant" who tried to rule over them. Since it was illegal for the nobles to try Darnley for treason, there were not too many options left.

The little prince, now six months old, was baptized a Catholic on December 17, at the chapel royal of Stirling Castle with as much splendor as was affordable. The queen clothed the nobility for the occasion. The procession from the royal apartments to the chapel was lit along the way by blazing torches. Inside the torch-lit chapel, the baby prince received the full sacrament, except that his mother drew the line at allowing a "pocky priest" to spit into her son's mouth. The Protestant lords stood outside in the cold winter air. A merry celebration with masques and fireworks followed.

All but the infant's father attended. Darnley was too fearful of further humiliation. On Elizabeth's orders, the English would never recognize him. And now, because of his behavior toward Mary, the French would not; the king's deportment, it was thought, was deplorable and incurable, and only promised to get much worse. Darnley had never appreciated against what opposition his wife had raised him to be king.

ON CHRISTMAS EVE, Mary yielded to pressures to sign the pardon for the earl of Morton, Darnley's worst enemy. The lion was let loose from his cage. Mary had to be turning her back, either unable to deal with the situation at all, or not wanting to know what was going to happen. She was too bright not to know something would, although everyone knew that she had always refused to be a part of any plot to kill her husband, no matter all his plots against her. As Darnley faced the prospect of confronting at last the men he betrayed, he fled to his family's stronghold in Glasgow. Rumors of plots and counterplots now abounded. Morton and his followers crossed the border from England in no time, and aligned in friendship with Bothwell and Mary's brother James. According to James Melville, "The days were evil and it was a busy time."

As the New Year began, Darnley became seriously ill with syphilis while staying at the family estates near Glasgow. Even while pursuing a way of ending their marriage, Mary's kind heart could not allow Darnley to suffer, and she sent her personal physician and some supplies to care for him. The word was, Darnley was suffering from smallpox, but how many people were fooled was questionable. Although seriously ill, rumors of Darnley's plots to win the crown by kidnapping his son and aligning with the Catholic hierarchy reached Mary. With Darnley in Glasgow, so close to his scheming father, Mary and her son were in greater danger. Fanned by his own father's political ambitions, Darnley's need to rule Scotland over Mary, as king, was an obsession fueled by pure ego, which made him extremely vulnerable to flattery, especially from his wife. So, when his wife went to Glasgow to collect him, he returned with her like a devoted puppy. On January 27, 1567, the royal couple left for Edinburgh, the king traveling by litter, a taffeta mask hiding his disfigured features.

Whether she had also convinced herself that this was her only solution is not clear, but she had Darnley believing they were reconciling. Given her abhorrence of violence and her repeated rejection of any plan that would cause her husband harm and her dishonor, it is highly unlikely that the purpose of the caravan was to hand Darnley over to his murderers. Against the wishes of his wife, who wanted him to convalesce at the castle of Craigmillar, just outside of Edinburgh but close by the little prince, Darnley chose instead to stay at the old provost's lodging at Kirk o'Field. Situated on a hill surrounded by gardens, the house was of moderate size and pleasant, and to Darnley, in his paranoia, may have felt safer than arriving in a place that was expecting him. On February 1, he was housed there to begin the "purging and cleansing of his sickness," before marital relations could resume. Although rushed because of the last-minute choice of lodgings, the furnishings brought for the king's comfort were elaborate and luxurious. A room for the queen was prepared on the floor below. If the queen had known of the imminent plan to murder the king by blowing the house up, it is doubtful she would have spent so much to feather his deathbed. A raven, which had followed the royal cortege from Glasgow, now perched itself on the roof of the king's last residence.

Just as his sickbed had brought them close originally, the royal couple again grew at least closer during what turned out to be the last week of Darnley's life. Mary found it difficult to sustain any kind of hard feelings in almost any situation. Whenever she had her husband all to herself—where he was not able to be influenced by others—he again became devoted to her. The king began to reveal some plots against her that he had learned about, and wrote his father that his health had greatly improved which he attributed to "the care of my love the Queen, who is behaving as a natural and loving wife. . . . I hope that God will lighten our hearts with joy that hath so long been afflicted with trouble." Mary spent her time between Holyrood, attending to business, and Kirk o'Field, attending to her husband.

One of the mysteries of Mary Stuart's life is whether or not she was aware of the developing plot by the nobles to assassinate the king. Unless she was a supreme actress and manipulator—which to this point she had never been accused of—Mary seemed to be growing fonder of her husband again and genuinely hopeful of a reconciliation. If she could somehow get him to grow up, she would have a partner she could trust, and perhaps the kingdom could begin to flourish in some kind of peace, as the nobles would not have the wedge of their marital troubles with which to promote their own interests.

The last Sunday before Lent, February 9, was crammed with social activities for the queen. After attending the last event, Mary and her nobles, except for her brother who always managed to slip out of town to avoid culpability, gathered in Darnley's rooms bringing with them the merriment of the day. All were still in their carnival costumes. The dark, Saturnine figure of Bothwell, splendid in black and silver, moved stealthily about the room like a panther. Great quantities of gunpowder had either already been laid down around the house, or soon would be. At around eleven o'clock, someone reminded the queen that she had promised to attend the masque held by her friend Bastian. Given the late hour, she changed her plans and decided to stay the night at Holyrood, rather than return to Kirk o'Field and the king. Her husband would be leaving for Holyrood early in the morning anyway. Darnley protested. He wanted her nearby that night. The queen took a small ring off her finger as a pledge of her intentions that they would be together permanently the next day.

Outside, the thin sliver of the new moon offered little light to dispel the blackness of the night. A thin film of snow covered the ground. For a moment, as she was readying herself to mount her horse to return to the castle, the queen noticed Bothwell's former servant French Paris in the torchlight. "Jesu, Paris," she remarked.

"How begrimed you are!"

By the time she returned, the wedding masque had nearly ended and it was time for the tradition of putting the bride to bed. Mary returned to her apartments with Bothwell and John Stewart of Traquair, the captain of her guard. Traquair left Mary and Bothwell, the man she now leaned on more than any other, alone. After Bothwell, excusing himself, went back to his apartments to change, he then made his way quietly back through the darkened alleyways of Edinburgh to supervise the lighting of the fuses at the king's residence. Mary retired peacefully to sleep. She could not have known what was about to happen, although many believed she was behind everything.

Darnley did not sleep. Instead, he asked for a bottle of wine and prepared for his five a.m. return to the castle. Sometime just before two in the morning, he and his servant either saw something or heard strange noises. Not taking a moment to think, they climbed out his window using a rope and a chair, carrying a dagger and wearing only a nightgown. Taylor, his servant, grabbed a furred robe.

Suddenly, a mighty explosion shattered the stillness of the night. All the citizens were startled awake. Queen Mary arose believing it was the sound of twenty-five or thirty cannons and sent for someone to investigate. Word came back that not one stone was left standing at Kirk o'Field, and that the king's body was found dead from strangulation in the garden sixty paces away.

Only two things were clear that night. Appalling violence had made the queen a widow, and Scotland was now plunged into a major political scandal. At least half the nobles were involved, and they were those closest to the queen, making her look extremely suspect to all but her closest friends. Death of the king by explosion was intended to cover tracks and not make one of the conspirators the scapegoat. Although he supervised the demolition, and nearly lost his life as he impatiently returned to the house when it seemed the fuses had not taken, Bothwell was not the one to commit the actual murder. No bruise or cut from falling rock had marred the king. A few of Douglas's men had noticed Darnley's escape and finished the job in the garden. Women from a cottage nearby claimed to have heard the king call out, "Pity me, kinsmen, for the sake of Jesus Christ who pitied all the world . . ." Darnley was not yet twenty-one.

Shock and horror were all Mary could feel at first. Clearly, she believed the assassins had intended to kill her as well, and it was "not chance but God Himself who had preserved her," as she had been so close to spending the night with the king. Her first reaction was to take "vigorous vengeance." "The matter is so horrible and strange," she wrote that same day to her ambassador in Paris, "as we believe the like was never heard of in any country . . . we hope to punish the same with such rigour as shall serve for example of this cruelty to all ages to come." This was when she believed the terrible murder was the work of her own enemies among the Protestants, before she came to understand it was the doings of those nobles she had counted as closest to her. "Fie, treason!" Bothwell exclaimed after being awakened from his brief sleep. As sheriff of Edinburgh, he gathered a few soldiers to accompany him on his inspection of the scene of the crime.

As the initial shock wore off, it seems a sort of numbness took over the queen of Scots. Since the birth of her son, she had fallen in and out of melancholy. Fearing a total breakdown, and "the great and imminent dangers of her health and life," as she commenced the forty days of mourning, her physician insisted she leave the horrible gloom of Edinburgh right away for the fresh air of the countryside, which had always been her antidote. Thus, she was reviled for playing golf and tennis five days after her husband's death, and became even more suspect.

But upon her return, she was facing the truth of her close nobles' involvement. The European leaders were asking for her to take action against the assassins, especially because not doing so was beginning to implicate her. Elizabeth wrote, urging Mary to preserve her honor and prove again to the world the noble princess that she was. "My ears have been so astounded and my heart so frightened to hear of the horrible and abominable murder of your husband and my cousin—that I have scarcely spirit to write; yet I cannot conceal that I grieve more for you than for him." Elizabeth had to make certain that Mary would not, in her desperation, return to the protection of France.

Amazing as it was that he didn't see it coming, the scheming nobles now made Bothwell the scapegoat. Placards declaring Bothwell the murderer and the queen as a result of witchcraft his accomplice, were springing up all over Edinburgh. One showed Mary, the woman who had been so recently their beloved queen, as a mermaid, naked from the waist up, a crown on her head, and next to her a hare, which was on Bothwell's crest. The two figures crouched in a circle of swords.

Mary uncharacteristically grew paralyzed with despair. Now she knew the plot was not against her, and that she was safe. Or was she? But whom could she turn to? Who was left to trust? Not one noble in her entire realm was without either guilt or a self-serving motive. Within a year, her secretary and then her husband had been brutally murdered by the people who surrounded her. Not only was she grieving them, but she was now grieving the loss of all hope of bringing peace to her country. Nothing had changed, or likely would. Her own mother had given her life to preserve Scotland for her daughter, and had died under the weight of so much useless and dangerous intrigue. Now she was to save the cruel kingdom for her son. What hope was there for such a barbarous country? In the face of such a disastrous and seemingly unsolvable situation, her great spirit deserted her. Her melancholy and despair grew until in March, Elizabeth's envoy found her "in a dark chamber, so as I could not see her face, but by her very words, she seemed very doleful, and did accept the sovereign's letters and messages in a very thankful manner . . ."[1]

Alone, of all the nobles, with his vigor and directness, the only dim light in all this darkness for the queen seemed Bothwell. Was it for herself that she would choose this coarse, crude womanizer with the strength and daring that she always greatly admired? Or did she believe that together they were the only hope for her country? Was it because of him that she would lose her crown, her liberty and her life, or was it that to lose all was her inevitable fate given the violent nature of the country she ruled?

Hillingford, Robert Alexander. Mary arriving at the Tower of London.
(Fine Art Photographic Library, London/Art Resource, NY)

Severn Joseph. Mary at
Loch Levern Castle.
(Victoria & Albert
Museum, London/Art
Resource, NY)

Hageman Mary D. (1882–1889). Mary being handed over to Elizabeth I's guards. Needlework picture, made in Princeton, NJ, 1882–1889.
(The Newark Museum/ Art Resource, NY)

Deveria, Eugene (1808–1865). Reading of the death sentence of Mary Stuart. 1826.
(Art Resource, NY)

12

Escape

A woman and her baby is the basic image of mythology.
—Joseph Campbell

Compelling Mary to give up her crown
separated the queen from her infant son,
sundering a primal bond akin to the all-absorbing,
if highly imaginary bond that Mary achieved with her subjects.
—Jayne Elizabeth Lewis

WHEN MARY ARRIVED at Stirling Castle on Monday, April 21, it had been six turbulent weeks since she had seen her son, Prince James, now ten months old. There was no way she could know, as she spent every moment of the next day playing with her baby and marveling at his development, that it would be the last time she would ever lay eyes on him, though she would live another nineteen years. Forgetting for a little while the fateful decisions she was having to soon make, this final sweet time together with her child, in the nursery of her own first five years, was the last truly happy, carefree day of her life. In the future, her son would only know her through the distorted filters of the people who surrounded him, all of whom had their own personal feelings about his legendary mother.

As if a part of her were preparing for the disaster that lay ahead, the next night, Mary sought the solace of the beautiful and peaceful palace of Linlithgow, the place of her birth. She awoke the next morning to return finally to Edinburgh. The date was April 24.

Nine years had passed since her marriage to Francois. Journeying back, Mary was accompanied by Maitland and two other nobles, and a small troop of thirty horsemen.

Some say she knew of the plan, some say she was unsuspecting, but when Bothwell suddenly appeared with an army of eight hundred at the Bridges of Almond, six miles from Edinburgh, claiming danger lay ahead for her in Edinburgh, this once imperious and spirited queen allowed him to take her horse by the bridle and turn her in the direction of the heart of Scotland and his castle of Dunbar forty miles away. Her little troop was no match for the strength of his troops, and the queen said she would comply in order to avoid any bloodshed.

Thus began what some called a bizarre rampage of self-destruction. What followed was so out of character that those who had always admired Mary's great virtue were stunned and accused Bothwell of casting a spell on her. Others believed the queen must have suffered from epilepsy, or porphyria, a form of madness that ran in her family genes, or from a nervous breakdown brought about by a guilty conscience. Romantics have claimed that suddenly awakened passions ran away with her. All agreed she acted with a total suspension of judgment. Her uncharacteristically docile manner as Bothwell took her horse's bridle made it seem as if her great spirit had left her completely. Some now believed she was a wicked woman, that her ensuing actions confirmed her complicity in the death of her husband the king.

Others blamed Bothwell. There could be no doubt that all month he had worked hard at clearing the path to Mary's bed and thus to her throne. On April 12, he stood trial and was absolved of Darnley's murder. Then on April 19, he threw a lavish feast at the Ainslie Tavern for twenty-eight of the nobles and prelates, and managed to persuade them all to sign what came to be known as the Ainslie Bond, that declared their approval of Bothwell as Mary's next husband. The bond stated they preferred that she marry Bothwell, a Scotsman, rather than a foreign prince. Only one minor obstacle remained. He was still married. Not one to let such a detail stand in his way, within a month, his marriage was quickly and amicably dissolved. Even with all his cunning, what he did not know, but should have prepared for, was that within hours of Darnley's murder, a well-orchestrated and deadly propaganda campaign was being directed at him by Mary's brother James and his cohorts Morton and Maitland. His ambition suddenly blinded him to the fact that they would abhor his bid for the same throne they coveted so desperately.

Although she had grown to trust Bothwell more than any of her other nobles, Mary was unnerved by the request of her nobles that she marry Bothwell, and refused at first, primarily because of the scandal that surrounded him. She was forced to consider it, though, since so many had signed the bond, and that gave her hope of peace among her nobles at last. She also knew full well that by herself, she was not strong enough to control any of them, and it was obvious that he could be the strong partner she so badly needed.

What is true is that, as she faced the supreme crisis of her life, Mary was physically weak, still recovering from childbirth, ill, dejected and without a true friend in her own country. The queen was easy prey for Bothwell's domination and blind ambitions. When news of her capture spread to Edinburgh the alarm bell of the city went off in an attempt to gather a force to rescue her. It was too late.

Many had been aware for over a week of Bothwell's plan to kidnap the queen, the stated purpose of which was to help Mary save face by seeming a victim. Although she may have complied with the plot, which was most likely presented to her by Bothwell's man, Black Ormiston, the night before, she had no idea that Bothwell planned to seal the deal by raping her. But that night, as the gates of Dunbar Castle were closed and locked behind her, Bothwell took possession of her body as well. Melville was convinced of it. "The Queen could not but marry him, seeing he had ravished her and lain with her against her will." In the queen's own words, "Albeit we found his doings rude, yet were his words and answers gentle."

Mary always claimed her marriage to Bothwell was for the benefit of the country, and that her heart was never given to him. She said she felt "keenly the perilous and damaging position in which I was placed. . . . Many things we revolved with ourself, but never could find an outgate." Now, "since it is past and cannot be brought back again, we will make the best of it."[1]

No one believed her. Queen Elizabeth was greatly scandalized and talked of having Prince James raised in England by his paternal grandmother. Catholic Europe openly despaired of Mary. The pope let it be known he would have nothing to do with the queen of Scots unless somehow she made a dramatic change. Protestant Europe was appalled. In France it was felt Mary behaved so ill that there was no hope of giving her help or advice.

There was no doubt as the days progressed that she was wholly committed to Bothwell, if not completely subdued and dominated by him. Mary did see in his strength hope for herself and Scotland against the constant treachery of the nobles. Compared with the rough Scottish nobles, very few of whom could sign their own name, Bothwell was a cultured man. He had spent time at the French court and could speak the language of Mary's youth with great facility. As well as having been a gentleman to the chamber of the king, he was a writer, author of several books, and owned an extensive collection.

But the hearts of her subjects were broken on May 6, as they watched their beautiful and once beloved and magical queen led back into Edinburgh by Bothwell, who again took hold of her horse's bridle as if she were his prize. On May 12, Mary returned to Bothwell the titles his ancestors once bore, duke of Orkney and lord of Shetland. Finally, on May 15, her fate was sealed. She married Bothwell in a Protestant service in the Great Hall of Holyrood. Only a little over three months had passed since the murder of her husband. In stark contrast to her two previous weddings, there was no pomp and only a wedding dinner for celebration. No gifts or tokens of love were exchanged between the couple.

If a spell had been cast, the wedding ceremony broke it. Or per-haps promises made of co-rulership were no longer kept. The next day Mary was in a flood of tears, repenting her actions, especially the betrayal of her Catholicism. She was overheard begging Arthur Erskine, her equerry, for a knife with which to kill herself, or else she would drown herself. Suspicious and jealous, Bothwell kept her heavily guarded day and night. His vile and abusive behavior toward her kept her in constant tears. His Protestant austerity despised her pleasure-loving nature. No longer was she permitted to dance, play music or even hunt. Her chamber door was even guarded, and no one was allowed in her presence unless Bothwell was there. Not a week had passed, and everyone in the court was exceedingly alarmed at the extraordinary and sudden change in her appearance.

Still Mary believed her marriage to Bothwell to be the only safeguard against the "frequent uproars and rebellions raised against us since we came in Scotland." She continued to explain that, "The travail thereof we may no longer sustain in our own person, being already wearied and almost broken." Bothwell immediately got to work to put the government in order, and his actions actually held great promise for the country. If they had been allowed time to work out their relationship, they may have left an impressive legacy. Alone of all her nobles, Bothwell's loyalty and support of Mary never wavered all the time they knew each other. Both dedicated to the cause of their country, their personal differences may have eventually worked themselves out. But even Bothwell was no match for the subversion of the nobles.

As TENSIONS GREW, Mary and Bothwell left on June 6 for Borthwick Castle, twelve miles south of Edinburgh, hoping to gather their forces. Mary melted Elizabeth's gold baptismal font to pay for the troops. Returning on June 11, from a disappointing recruiting campaign, Bothwell found the castle under siege and escaped, leaving Mary to hold the castle. The insurgents called for the queen to leave her husband and return with them to Edinburgh. When she refused, they shouted disgusting insults at her. In the dead of night, the queen, dressed in men's clothes, booted and spurred, escaped and rode to meet her husband. Together, they made their way under the cover of the black sky to the coastal fortress of Dunbar Castle.

Lured by promises of protection in his safeguarded Edinburgh Castle by the Judas, Balfour, Mary and Bothwell left the safety of Dunbar. Having only the costume she wore during her escape, Mary borrowed a red petticoat that was too short for her, a muffler and a velvet hat, and sleeves tied with bows as was the fashion. She also was pregnant with Bothwell's child. Although her beauty and allure was undiminished by her hastily put-together ensemble, in Mary's words, "The people did not join as expected." Propaganda against her by Knox and the rebel nobles had undermined her. Mary was now seen by many of her subjects as an "abandoned creature." Where her reputation before Bothwell and after her imprisonment was impeccable, for the six months she was with him, she was said by Knox and Buchanan—the man who would be supervising the education of her son—to be "foul as a leper." What would turn out to be their last night together was spent at Seton, the house Mary had loved most during her six-year reign.

On June 15, an intensely hot day, the ragtag royal army met the rebels on Carberry Hill. The rebel army flaunted a banner showing an almost naked body of Darnley lying under a tree, his infant son James kneeling beside him holding a scroll which read, "Judge and avenge my cause, O Lord." There was no battle at Carberry Hill.

Lacking any real leader, the nobles recruited du Croc, the French ambassador, to persuade Mary to leave Bothwell, promising they would remain her loyal subjects. Mary reacted with fury. "It was by them that Bothwell had been promoted," Mary repeated over and over. Individual challenges to fight were made to Bothwell, but none followed through. As the fierce warrior stood defiant, what was hardly an army began to slither away and return home. Bothwell proposed to Mary that they return to Dunbar, but she wanted to avoid bloodshed. Trusting in their honor and believing she would be respectfully treated, Mary surrendered to the lords at eight in the evening, on the condition that Bothwell could leave the field unmolested.

In the summer dusk, before both armies, the couple embraced for what would be the last time, and Bothwell with thirty companions took the eastward road to Dunbar. His power had lasted five weeks only. Before leaving, Bothwell pressed into Mary's hand the bond that implicated Maitland and Morton in Darnley's murder. Husband and wife would never lay eyes on each other again.

Still wearing the borrowed outfit with the short red petticoat, now spattered with mud, Mary was escorted back to Edinburgh; the banner of her dead husband, her son kneeling beside his father, led the procession. Along the way, the mob yelled out, "Burn the whore! Kill her! Drown her! She is not worthy to live!" Knox had kept the public furious. "The queen had no more liberty to commit murder and adultery than the average person." He predicted a great plague from God on the whole nation if she were not punished. Mary Stuart, queen of Scots, was utterly alone. Having always been greatly loved by her subjects, she was stunned by their insults. She could not hide her tears of hurt, humiliation and shock from the taunts of her tormentors who lined the road.

Instead of taking her to her own quarters, the rebels housed her in the home of the provost of Edinburgh. While the rebels ate a hardy supper, Mary retreated to the room the nobles provided, which was far below her station. She was provided with nothing, and had no privacy as the guards remained, to her horror, in her bedroom with her. The reality of the nobles' deceit and betrayal did not take long to realize. Outside her window was the malicious accusing banner, displayed for her benefit. As she searched for hope outside her window, she spotted Maitland, her first and most indispensable advisor to whom she had bestowed so much—her very last hope. She called out to him, but he slouched by pretending not to hear her.

Desperate by the next morning, this once exquisite and virtuous beauty, hailed a goddess by poets all over Europe, stood framed by the window, her red petticoat now torn to her waist, breasts exposed, auburn hair loose, pleading with her subjects to rescue her from the rapacious nobles who betrayed her. Her appeals to their loyalty were met with mockery and jeers from the rioting crowd outside. But, as she remained standing before them, so utterly vulnerable and seared with despair, they remembered again all she had meant to them, and pity replaced their scorn.

Realizing that if she stayed longer among her subjects, their queen would win back their love, the nobles imprisoned her in Lochleven, a castle owned by Sir William Douglas built on one of the four islands contained within the loch. She was not allowed to take any clothes, not even a nightdress, nor anyone other than two maids with her. Believing at first that she was going to be taken to Stirling to be with her son, she did not protest. The two nobles she most despised, Ruthven and Lindsay, were her escorts. At some point during the fifty-mile trip north, she learned of a plot by the Hamiltons to rescue her. To give them a chance, she tried to slow the pace, but her horse was whipped and spurred on. As she was finally rowed across the desolate waters of the loch, Mary's spirit gave out. For over two weeks, she remained nearly comatose in the laird's room, not eating, drinking, or speaking to anyone, and those around her worried she may soon die. The queen was seven weeks pregnant.

Her pregnancy put her life in great peril—not physically, but because the nobles were asking her to renounce Bothwell or remain imprisoned, and because of her pregnancy she would not. If she were to renounce him, her child would be considered a bastard. Rather than that, Throckmorton reported to Elizabeth that Mary vowed she would "live and die with him, and sayeth if it were but her choice to relinquish her crown and kingdom or the Lord Bothwell, she would leave her kingdom and dignity to live as a simple damsel with him." Perhaps her feelings for Bothwell were deepening with the pregnancy, but it was more likely she was thinking of the well-being of her child, rather than speaking from any great passion for her husband. For the next two months, her husband valiantly attempted to gather enough political and military support to free Mary, but it was just not there. Survival in Scotland meant aligning with whomever was in power—or lands, castles and lives could be quickly and brutally lost. Bothwell and the queen of Scots were bereft of power.

MARY MISCARRIED TWINS, and as she lay weak from serious bleeding, the nobles approached her asking her to resign her crown. Despite her utterly vulnerable position, the queen reacted with outrage, not just for herself, but for the idea and the precedent that subjects could hold their ruler prisoner and control the crown. Her neighbor Elizabeth threatened the lords should they touch a hair on

Mary's head, which is probably the reason she was still alive. Elizabeth had no real sympathy for Mary personally. The threat, however, of a serious, international crises, and the threat to the institution of the monarchy, was uppermost in her mind. Throckmorton did not believe his negotiations and threats on behalf of Elizabeth could keep Mary alive much longer. He could see how easily she could go the same violent way as Riccio and Darnley.

Despite her vehement and courageous refusals, in the end, Mary was forced under extreme duress to relinquish her crown to her young son. Her brother James would act as regent. Immediately, she fell ill again and believed this time she had been poisoned. On July 29, her young son, now thirteen months old, was crowned King James VI of Scotland. As bonfires were lit and canons discharged in celebration on the little island, Mary wept.

When her brother at last paid her a visit at Lochleven, Mary's hopes of his kindness were dashed. James took a righteous stand and lectured her about all her errors of judgment, and at one point threatened her with execution for Darnley's death. Mary never appreciated how little James ever cared for her, and how very much he resented being the illegitimate sibling with no claims to the crown, despite being their father's firstborn and a son. His whole life was spent usurping her power. Now, he stole most of her jewels and valuables as well. He was a deceptive figure, presenting to the world a certain uprightness, when in truth his actions stemmed from resentment and his motives were entirely self-serving.

Bothwell had by August fled Scotland, but then landed in prison in Norway, caught by creditors and the family of his former mistress. For a while, he was used as a political pawn. But when his value did not seem worth the trouble, he lived the rest of his life in a series of ever-worsening prisons, until he died insane, after being tied to a stake for ten years in a horrible dungeon within the pitiless fortress of Dragsholm. No records show if Mary asked much about him after awhile.

By October, Mary's health had returned, and she began to win over everyone on the little island with her charm and fun-loving nature, especially the young and dashing George Douglas, half brother to Mary's brother James, who was besotted by her. The peace and tranquility, after the virtual hell of the last two years, revived her spirit and renewed her physically. Even so, all were aware she was like a lioness pacing her cage, waiting for a chance to escape.

Her peace was not to last long. By December, she was formally accused of the murder of her husband, by the very men who were guilty of the crime, and who were now the men ruling her country. Her brother refused her a public hearing. By spring, she had figured out a way to smuggle letters to the queens of France and England, but she was ever as anxious for the well-being of her accomplices as for herself.

In her first escape attempt, Mary disguised herself as a laundress. But the legendary white beauty of her hands betrayed her. The boatman rowing the women away from shore grew suspicious about why this one laundress refused to show her face. When he reached to pull off her hood, Mary instinctively reached with her hands to protect herself, and that was when the boatman knew he was transporting the queen of Scots. Wanting no part of such responsibility, he rowed her back to the shore of her prison. But he kept her secret.

The constant possibility of her escaping was in the very air they all breathed on the tiny island. During a boating excursion, some played a joke that she had indeed escaped, which was unfortunately taken seriously. In the ensuing commotion, Mary's surgeons were needed to attend to the wounded along the shore.

When on Sunday, May 2, the inevitable happened and Mary finally did make her escape, it was with the help of George Douglas and his orphaned cousin Willy Douglas. While Willy pegged all the boats, except one, to prevent their pursuit, the queen feigned a fainting spell to distract the laird of the castle, who was becoming suspicious of Willy's actions down by the shore. When the laird went to his supper, Mary excused herself to go pray in her own rooms and changed into the clothes of a chambermaid. Distracting the laird, George was able to get the keys to the castle and all was ready. He bid his mother farewell. They all believed he was leaving for France. At his signal, the queen strode boldly, in her disguise, across the courtyard and through the gate. When the coast was clear, she climbed into the boat and curled up under the boatman's seat to avoid detection and possible cannon fodder. Washerwomen along the shore spotted the queen, but kept mum.

Arriving on the far shore, Mary was greeted by George Douglas. Mounting a fine horse stolen from the stables of the laird of Locheven himself, the queen rode off to meet Lord Seton, accompanied only by Willy. After ten and a half months of captivity, the queen of Scots was finally free. As she road on to Seton's palace, country folk along the way cheered their heroic queen on. Mary's heart must have soared at the sound. The old magic was at work again.

In less than a week, her devotees again appeared to support her cause. Aided by the Hamiltons who never let go of their own ancient claim to the throne and virulently resented Mary's brother James, she drew to her a larger army than her brother's. As the two forces met, though, Mary soon learned that her numbers were inadequate to the military leadership of her brother's. At one point, Mary road into the midst of the battle and eloquently tried to rally her troops. But she discovered her troops were actually hopeless, and any effort to lead them in battle would have been wasted, as all they were doing was fighting among themselves. The results now obvious, Mary fled for her life.

Across the most primitive terrain, with no provisions and little time, Mary scarcely stopped for food or sleep until she reached the south of Scotland where her Catholic supporters could offer protection. Her dramatic flight is best described by Mary's own words in a letter to her uncle in France: "I have endured injuries, calumnies, imprisonment, famine, cold, heat, flight not knowing whither, ninety-two miles across the country without stopping or alighting, and then I have had to sleep on the ground and drink sour milk, and eat oatmeal without bread, and have been three nights like the owls . . ."

Toward the end of her life, she reflected on her fatal decision to seek refuge in England, rather than in France where she was still their treasured queen dowager, or remaining longer under the protection of her Catholic subjects in Scotland: "But I commanded my best friends to permit me to have my own way . . ."

Presumably her friends tried to persuade her to take the safer course, which was the protection of France. As she contemplated a comfortable and predictable life at the French court, that part of Mary that was so courageous and noble must have caused her to wonder if she would wither and die in such a predetermined life. Also, throughout her troubles in Scotland, it had been Elizabeth, and not even her Guise uncles in France, who seemed to care and respond. Why would they send an army for her now, when they hadn't before? Mary unfortunately could not see that Elizabeth's motivations were primarily political survival for her own self, and not based on any true fondness for her cousin. And so there was hope that, if she could just meet with Elizabeth, she could persuade her to see her side and join forces to win her throne back. An alliance with England would not only keep her in line for succession, but advance her son's interests as well. At that moment in time, Mary gambled on herself, rather than quit the game.

Mary sheared off her long golden-red hair to prevent any chance that she might be recognized. Still, as a precaution, a hood was an essential element to her borrowed disguise. In this costume, on Sunday May 16, after attending Mass at the exquisite twelfth-century Cistercian abbey of Dundrennan, Mary Queen of Scots stood on the seashore of Solway Firth and gazed at the distant shores of England. At three o'clock that afternoon, with a small party accompanying her, Mary climbed into a crude little boat used for inshore fishing and carrying coals and lime across the Solway Firth. Mary Queen of Scots left behind the shores of her kingdom, never to return.

Midway through the four-hour crossing, while contemplating the approaching shore, Mary suddenly had a strong vision of the future that lay before her in England, and immediately commanded the boatman to take her to nearby France instead. But the unequivocal tides made such a change in her tragic fate impossible, and relentlessly carried her on toward English shores, and nearer to her destiny at Fotheringhay.

13

Captive Queen

His Higness told me the deathe of the Queen his mother
was visible in Scotland before it did really happen
being, as he said, spoken of in secrete
by those whose power of sighte presentede to them
a bloodie heade dancinge in the aire.

—*Sir John Harington*

THAT EVENING, the twenty-four-year old queen of Scots landed at Workington, a small fishing port near the mouth of the River Derwent. Any trepidation from her premonition was allowed to drift away with the tide, as Mary stepped out of the boat and onto English soil, elated and excited. Her hooded costume fooled no one in the little village. The Scottish queen's legendary beauty could not be disguised, and the villagers crowded around in curiosity and awe.

As soon as she landed, Mary wrote the queen of England a long letter documenting everything that had happened to her since Riccio's death, and how now she was left with nothing in the world but the borrowed clothes on her back. She begged Elizabeth to send for her.

Elizabeth's first instinct was to welcome Mary to the court, offering to help restore her to the Scottish throne if she promised not to align with France. She warned her Scottish cousin, "Those who have two strings to their bow may shoot stronger, but they rarely shoot straight." No welcome was to be forthcoming, though. Elizabeth was overruled by the majority of her counselors, including Cecil, who along with the others was aligned with Mary's Protestant brother James. They demanded Mary's name be cleared of complicity in Darnley's murder, lest the meeting would besmirch their queen's reputation.

The consummate manipulator, Elizabeth always managed to appear innocent and unassailable while having her way. Maitland had advised the bishop of Ross never to trust the word of the queen of England, "for you will find all plain craft without true dealing." Instead of believing the queen of Scots on the subject of her husband's murder, Elizabeth chose to believe James, even though he, too, had been implicated in the crime. Instead of an invitation, Elizabeth sent Mary her first keeper, the outspoken and highly moral Frances Knollys.

A Reformationist, Knollys believed, "Dominion belonged to men, not to women; God ordained it so." Knollys found Mary to be "every bit as passionate and intense as the Queen of England, yet without Elizabeth's restraining wariness of action." In his opinion, the queen of Scots "played her highness with thunderings and great countenances." Complaining of the shabby gowns she was provided, Mary felt they were only "fit coverings for saddles." When appealed to, what Elizabeth sent from her own wardrobe was so stingy and worn as to be completely embarrassing, even to Knollys, who explained away the shameful treatment by lying that they had been intended for Mary's maids. Her brother James was even less generous. It seemed no one wanted Mary to feel or look like a queen.

Thankfully, Mary Seton, the last of the Maries, arrived with her exceptional talents as a hairdresser, which was needed more than ever, since Mary had cropped her hair short during her escape. She would remain with her queen and childhood companion until Mary's death. The appreciative Knollys could not get over Seton's skill, writing: "Among other pretty devices, yesterday and today she did set such a curled hair upon the Queen that it was like to be a periwig that showed very delicately; and every other day she hath a new device of head dressing, without any cost, and yet setteth forth a woman gaily well."

In a letter to Elizabeth's right-hand advisor, Cecil, Knollys reported that Mary's "sheer physical energy and implacable determination to defeat her enemies made her truly dangerous," although, as he got to know Mary better, he began to admire her greatly. "The thing that most she thirsteth after is victory, so for victory's sake, pain and perils seem pleasant to her and in respect of victory, wealth and all other things seem to her contemptible and vile." In her semi-captivity at Carlysle Castle, Knollys watched the queen of Scots as she rode out to hunt, galloping at breakneck speed, and could easily imagine the legends of her rushing to the head of her troops, inspiring her soldiers to overcome their weariness. He observed that courage and valor were qualities she most admired in others. Clearly, the English had a lot on their hands with their exotic and uninvited guest.

As her charms drew him in despite himself, Knollys found Mary to have an "eloquent tongue and a discreet head, with stout courage and a liberal heart adjoined there unto." He was struck by the fact that Mary never put herself at a higher station than others, but spoke to commoners and nobles with equal respect and sincerity. Men began to flock to meet the queen of Scots, and all fell under her spell. Knollys began to worry that Mary may be weaving a web of conspiracy with so much support around her. Her devotee, George Douglas, stayed within the castle walls, and a growing number of friends rallied to her side, staying in town. Her movements, though guarded by a hundred men, were not yet restricted.

Worried about his ability to keep such a rare and delightful bird long in her cage, Knollys' concern about her influence grew. Mary being the "very pith and marrow of sweet eloquence would continue to attract followers wishing for her to have the crown of England upon her head."[1] Although it is doubtful that Mary personally had such designs, as she always only spoke about the issue of succession for herself and her son, it was certain her Catholic followers in England and Scotland were already conspiring. It began to seem she was even more trouble to England than to Scotland. As her threat grew, Knolleys was charged with holding Mary prisoner, while getting her to believe she was a guest. His concerns were great, as he knew her courage would allow her to climb from her bedroom window if need be.

All Mary wanted was to meet Elizabeth. Knowing her great powers of persuasion, Mary knew she could win Elizabeth to her cause should they ever meet. During the summer, Mary wrote over twenty letters appealing to her dear cousin, as well as letters to Spain and France asking for aid. But the queen of England grew concerned about the risk of the charming Mary winning over her own court. Elizabeth continued to promise hope of a meeting, while secretly conspiring with Mary's enemies to keep her imprisoned. Her greatest and lifelong understandable fear, that Mary had designs upon her throne, grew the longer "the Scottish enchantress" remained in her realm. With Mary imprisoned, her Protestant enemies—who, because of their own inability to do so, could not imagine Mary maintaining freedom of religion for both Catholics and Protestants—felt safer with her confined. Without her leadership, the Catholics were again being horribly persecuted in both countries. At this point the queen of Scots was a wild card in the delicate balance of diplomacy with the European countries. Because they could not be trusted, no one could trust the already-proven guileless leadership of Mary Stuart.

In a poem to Elizabeth that summer, Mary describes, in effect, the hope and the doubt she would play out for the next nineteen years in her ever-deepening imprisonment, against the subversion of her brother and the paranoia of the English queen.

A longing haunts my spirit, day and night
Bitter and sweet, torments my aching heart
'Twixt doubt and fear, it holds its wayward part,
And while it lingers, rest and peace takes flight . . .

Ah! I have seen a ship freed from control
On the high seas, outside a friendly port,
And what was peaceful change to woe and pain:
Ev'n so am I, a lonely trembling soul,
Fearing—not you, but to be made the sport

Of Fate, that bursts the closest, strongest chain.[2]

In mid-July, on learning that she was to be removed from the border to greater security at Bolton Castle, an isolated stronghold on the Yorkshire moors, Mary was beginning to become aware that she was actually a prisoner of the queen of England, and reacted with tears, tantrums, then suddenly graceful acquiesce. Still, she remained firmly against allowing her royal status to be submitted to a court. She would not even submit to Elizabeth's judgment unless allowed to meet her. Instead, Elizabeth threw it to the Scottish Parliament and Mary's brother, now occupying the throne as regent, to prove Mary's innocence.

The Scottish lords knew that Elizabeth did want to see Mary reinstated on the throne or at least returned to Scotland in some capacity, and Elizabeth must have known how much they would resist that prospect with all their might. Embarking on a campaign to thoroughly blacken the queen of Scots' reputation, James, Morton and others brought out the infamous silver casket letters they had discovered in Bothwell's quarters four days after Mary had parted from Bothwell. Nothing had been made of the discovery until now, when suddenly the letters were found to thoroughly implicate the queen. Never mind that the letters were for the most part forgeries and discernible lies, the alleged contents eclipsed Mary's chances of ever gaining her freedom, and were shamelessly used by all her enemies to keep her imprisoned for the rest of her life.

All of her life Mary Stuart was destined to be a victim to the ambition, the hatreds and the fears of others. Now this spirited twenty-five-year-old daughter of a king and queen, twice-anointed queen herself of two different countries, to whom freedom had been as essential as breathing, faced a life of ever-increasing restrictions, ever-worsening conditions, a life varied for the most part only by changes of residence, degrees of health and sickness, raised and then dashed hopes of rescue and fewer and fewer visitors. She never stopped advocating for herself, and not until the very end did she give up. That would be, though, when she would finally triumph gloriously over all her enemies.

DURING THE LONG, dark days of the first winter of her captivity, Mary paced and fumed in her confinement and hated her tedious inactivity. When Knollys first told her she was being moved again, Mary threatened she would have to be "bound hand and foot" first. Feeling vulnerable and helpless, Mary felt keenly Elizabeth's betrayal, and began to believe Elizabeth planned to take over her son and Scotland. But on January 26, with an "evil will and much ado," Mary left for the estates of her next jailer, Shrewsbury, further away from Catholic or Scottish support. The journey was a nightmare of bad roads, foul weather, much illness and many misunderstandings. Their destination, Tutbury Castle, was a large dilapidated medieval castle, vulnerable to every wind that blew and primarily used as a hunting lodge. No longer was there any doubt she was a prisoner.

For the next fifteen years, George Talbot, sixth earl of Shrewsbury, a wealthy nobleman of high station and character, and his famous second wife, Bess of Hardwick, would serve as her jailers. They tried to make Mary feel as comfortable as possible. Tapestries and Turkish carpets were used to block the drafts, which in the wintertime were horrendous. Most of the furnishings were of gold and crimson satin fabric. The queen was served on a silver plate, and she sat on a royal dais beneath a cloth of state. Although completely opposite in nature, Bess and Mary formed a friendship, and created a great deal of their now-famous needlework over the years while they passed together the "irksome restraints and weary monotony of her days." Toward the end of their relationship, Bess, twenty years her elder, would falsely accuse Mary of seducing her husband.

In the beginning as they adjusted to each other, Shrewsbury relayed to Cecil: "She is most offended at my restraining her from walking without the castle." Mary received many visitors from all over. Visiting Jesuits upon meeting her commented, "It is impossible to see this excellent queen without rapture and celestial joy." She was still allowed her music, walks in the garden, archery, riding and hawking. Shrewsbury would always be criticized, sometimes furiously by Elizabeth, for being too lenient with Mary, allowing her much more freedom than the queen of England had in mind for her.

Small animals, especially dogs and birds, had always been kept by the queen of Scots as lovingly tended pets, and became even more important to her during her years of imprisonment. In a letter to the archbishop of Glasgow, her ambassador to Paris, she wrote: "I beg you procure me pigeons, and red partridges and hens from Barbary. I intend to endeavor to rear them in this country, or to feed them in cages as I do all the small birds I can come by, a pastime for a prisoner. The only pleasure I have is in all the small animals I can procure."

In all the years of her imprisonment, Mary never lost interest in fashion. In addition to the birds, she also requested the archbishop send her "patterns of dresses and samples of cloths gold silver and silver stripe, the fittest and rarest now worn at court." She also ordered a couple of coifs with gold and silver crowns to be made at Poissy, and from Italy the "newest kinds of head-gear, veils, and bands with gold and silver."

However, for the rest of her life Mary's waking hours would be filled with the constant sound of the tramp of a large number of armed guards in the gardens below her windows, outside her doors and around the castles, so that "unless she transforme herself into a flea or a mouse, it was impossible that she should escape."

Outside her large casement windows at Tutbury, the River Dove meandered through the wide-open countryside, where cattle grazed. A simple village clustered about the castle walls, and behind the castle were the dense woods of the Derbyshire Hills. Frequent changes of residence occurred with the need to periodically thoroughly clean the present quarters.

Chartley had no expansive view like Tutbury. In fact, there was an oppressive stillness to the Chartley castle. A lake graced the foot of the lawn. The castle was surrounded by a moat, and Mary was allowed to cross over a little bridge and wend her way through a grove of trees. Twice, since Mary's stay there, Chartley nearly burned to the ground. However, the tiny room overlooking the moat, which served as Mary's bedchamber, was miraculously spared each time. Another of Shrewsbury's homes was Sheffield, her home off and on for fourteen years. Long, straight avenues of oak and walnut led up to the house. The pristine land, with herds of deer and flocks of rare birds, covered four acres of noble trees and was surrounded by rivers. In the winter, chilling blasts of wind blew from the bleak moors.

Barely a day would go by that Mary did not dream of her deliverance. Plots to free her were constantly finding their way to her by secret means. Most she would wisely ignore. A few seriously entangled her, despite her denials of being a part of any plot. She knew her only real hope was through the crowned heads of Europe, with whom she was in constant correspondence. Although the Catholics and her Guise relations considered many solutions, real help never came. Finally, "hope deferred maketh the heart sick." With his exalted guest the focus of so many intrigues, Shrewsbury had much on his hands. At one point he complained that "it nearly brought him to his grave."

MARY LONGED FOR the day that her son, now King James VI of Scotland, could intervene on her behalf, which she believed a son would naturally do for his mother. From the time of her arrival in England, Mary made anxious attempts to remain in contact with her child. Known for her love of children, Mary missed her little boy terribly. When he was four and a half, she sent him a little pony and a saddle, with a note: "Dear Son, I send three bearers to see you and bring me word how we do, and to remember you that ye have in me a loving mother that wishes you to learn in time to love, know and fear God." Mary's prayer was that he would not forget "anent her that has born you in her sides." Elizabeth never allowed the gifts or the letter out of England.

Instead, the English queen approached the Scottish government about the possibility of raising James in England, an idea that thrilled Mary. In her enthusiasm, Mary wrote to her former mother-in-law who had stayed involved with James, seeking her advice as grandmother: "I have born him and God knoweth with what danger to him and to me both, and of you he is descended, so I mean not to forget my duty to you." But the Scottish lords refused to allow their king to be reared in England, despite the hope he would someday rule England as well as Scotland. Mary continued to appeal to Elizabeth to, if not allow her to correspond, at least receive some word about his well-being. Mary beseeched Elizabeth, as a "desolate mother whose solitary child has been torn from her arms." Her pleas landed on deaf ears.

If he could not be close to her, Mary wished for her son to be raised and educated in France by her Guise relations, as she had been. She wanted more than anything to counteract the hostile influences that surrounded him. James' senior tutor, the severe Presbyterian, George Buchanan, was a staunch enemy of Mary's, and James was brought up to know that his mother was responsible for the murder of his father. In such a stern atmosphere, James developed into a highly intellectual and well-educated young man, a true scholar, but all of his life he would crave love, which became his downfall. Physically, he did not inherit his parents' good looks or their height, but he did develop the same intense love of horses and outdoor sport as his mother, as well as her enjoyment of a glamorous court life. Like Mary, he surrounded himself with poets and musicians when he grew older. Although reared Protestant, much to Mary's heartbreak, James early on developed a strong interest in the occult. As is seen especially with her needlework, another gift she tried to send him, her love for puns was also enjoyed by her son.

Mary believed her son loved her, as she had loved her mother though apart from her. "Everyone assures me that my son recognizes infinitely his duty towards me and that the poor chylde dare not show it in the captivity he is in."

When he turned eleven, James became aware of Bothwell's confession, exonerating Mary of any complicity in his father's murder, and wrote:

Whereas grievous accusations and calumnies have been all along impressed upon me against her majesty, my mother, this day I have seen a manifest declaration of her innocence.

Mary was overjoyed to learn of her son's reaction. More than anything, Mary wanted to get her son out of the hands of the ruthless regent Morton, the most instrumental in Darnley's death, and the quickest to lie about Mary to her son. Morton had not spared James the sight of the brutal death of his grandfather Lennox, who ruled as regent before Morton's ascension. Always an Anglophile, Morton had Elizabeth's complete support. When in May 1573, the castle of Edinburgh, in the hands still of Marians, fell with the support of the English, Mary's hopes of being returned to Scotland were lost. Elizabeth obviously never had such an intention.

Neither did she intend for mother and son to ever be close. When James wrote Mary an affectionate letter apologizing for being unable to receive her gifts, it was intercepted and retained by Elizabeth. Only when, in 1580, Mary's bitter enemy Morton fell from power was she able to receive her son's letters. In the letters written lovingly, James expressed the hope that in time he would be entirely "at her devotion."

A year later, Morton was executed, and Mary proposed an alliance of co-rulership between mother and son. "Given the compulsory abdication at Lochleven could not be considered legal, the regal power could not really belong to James. But, she would legalize his authority, if he would acknowledge her as the lawful sovereign of Scotland and would unite her name with his in the conduct of affairs."[3] The idea thoroughly alarmed Elizabeth, who feared losing support against Spain.

Mother-and-son negotiations were interrupted with the Raid of Ruthven in 1582. In another English victory, James, now sixteen, was made a prisoner for a year. Still, he managed to write his mother:

> Be assured that in all the adversities I have sustained for love of you, I have never failed of, nor been turned from my duty and affection toward you, but, on the contrary, they augment with every trouble that befalls me. Always, I would show that I recognize my duty towards you as much as any son in the world towards his mother.

In 1583, the young Prince James escaped from the Ruthven conspirators, unscathed and stronger.

RELIGIOUS CIVIL WARS ravaged France and the Netherlands. As the English heard stories of atrocities from the Dutch, Flemish and Huguenot refugees, they feared for their own way of life, for their future peace and prosperity, and that of their children, newly-won under Elizabeth's rule. The Guises were in the thick of the revolt, and Mary became guilty by association.

Then a smuggled copy of the Papal Bull *Regnans in Excelsis* was nailed to the door of the bishop of London's palace in St. Paul's Church, revealing to the citizens that Pope Pius V had finally excommunicated Elizabeth, "the Servant of Wickedness." The pope presumed to deprive Elizabeth of her false title to her throne, and absolved her Catholic subjects from their duty of allegiance to her.

Durham Cathedral was stormed and every symbol of Anglican worship was destroyed or defaced, and the cathedral was restored to Catholicism. High Mass was said as the soldiers stood by. Catholics by the hundreds sought absolution for the excommunication they brought onto themselves by conforming to official Protestantism. This was treason against the queen of England. It was Mary's presence in England, whether or not she lifted a finger in support, that gave England's Catholics heart. Over a hundred thousand Catholics, with centuries-old religious sentiments and ancient desires for revenge, had been slumbering.

It is highly doubtful that Mary approved of any violent overthrow, given her history of tolerance and her abhorrence of violence. At the end of her life, she said she would have gladly given up the throne if it would ensure tolerance of Catholics, and only wished to be an inspiration to convert others to her faith. Mary did seriously consider marrying the most prominent Catholic, the thirty-one-year-old duke of Norfolk, heir to a great name and a huge fortune, which would have made her extremely powerful. Because of their association, Mary was implicated in a plot against Elizabeth, although Mary was actually only interested in his assistance with regaining her own throne.

The Spanish, Italian and French governments supported the restoration of Catholicism in England, and the queen of Scots to her throne if not also to the throne of England. Fear was inflamed by Elizabeth's advisors, and Norfolk was eventually executed for treason in what was known as the Ridolphi Plot. The possibility exists that the plot was really set up by Cecil to destroy Mary and Norfolk. The English, though not as savage as the Scots, were every bit as treacherous.

The elimination of Mary Stuart was long overdue as far as Elizabeth's advisors and a committee representing both houses of Parliament were concerned. They called for Elizabeth to "cut off her head and make no more ado about her, that notorious whore, adulteress, and murderess, that monstrous and huge dragon that menaced England's peace and security, the lodestar of rebellion and treachery and danger from abroad."[4]

Mary "ceased to be regarded as a rather forlorn figure, a queen torn from her throne, a mother separated from her child, a vivacious prisoner to be secretly pitied, to an ungrateful bosom serpent, a papist snake in the grass of the English Eden, irrevocably associated in the popular imagination with subversion, treachery, and bloody murder."[5] "All men now cry out against your prisoner," Lord Burghley told the Earl of Shrewsbury. "If the sore be not salved," warned Francis Walsingham, referring to religious persecutions in France and Italy, "I fear we shall have a Bartholomew breakfast or a Florence banquet. Her head should be chopped off forthwith."

Elizabeth was torn. She listened as her advisors called Mary an "irritated tyrant, traitorous and pestilence of Christendom." To execute Mary, they argued, would be to "save Elizabeth's own blood, and her dearest counselors' blood, and the blood of the whole realm." The cousins' true blood tie had to become less important to Elizabeth than ties of "figurative" blood, before the blood of the queen of Scots could be spilled.

Increasingly, Elizabeth required stricter control of Mary's imprisonment and her health was being severely affected. When Mary was returned to Tutbury, after Shrewsbury's dismissal, she was given only two rooms for all of her lodgings, in the old castle built of wood, full of holes and tumbling down on all sides. Mary described her living conditions in a letter: "Here the sun can never penetrate, neither does any pure air visit this habitation, on which descend drizzling damps and eternal fogs, to such excess, that not an article of furniture can be placed beneath the roof, but in four days it becomes covered in green mold." Mary went on to say that the rooms appeared more suited to the housing of the "vilest criminals." No one should endure such conditions. At night, it was intensely cold and everyone was sick. Her physician preferred not to remain any longer. As further insult, she had no real "cabinet," or bathroom. One-quarter acre only, and not even fit for a swine, was set aside for exercise. Death and sickness were all around. To intimidate and cruelly punish her, a poor priest was tortured for his faith and hung outside her window.

Exercise and the outdoors were as essential as breathing to Mary all her life. When she was restricted to walks in the dining room or in a tiny courtyard, Mary became unable to leave her room for weeks, growing increasingly weak and ill. The pain in her side, which had developed many years before, nearly disabled her now. Finally, she became so debilitated that her servants had to carry her from room to room. "And to speak still more freely, necessity making me, to my regret, overcome shame," Mary writes, "I began to be very ill attended to my own person, and with no regard to my infirm state." Believing she had passively endured her confinement and complied in every way she knew how, she was amazed that they would want to "hasten by evil and unworthy treatment that which they do not wish or are unable to execute otherwise, lest they make themselves openly culpable."

IN 1580, AS SHE BECAME overwhelmed with humiliation and misery from her long confinement, the harsh and inhumane treatment more suited to the barbaric methods of the Dark Ages than the end of the sixteenth century, and the failure to effect her freedom, she wrote in her "Essay on Adversity," on the lives of rulers: "Tribulation has been to them as a furnace of fine gold—a means of improving their virtue, of opening their so-long-blinded eyes, and of teaching them to know themselves and their own failings."

Mary wrote this essay believing she now understood adversity so well, and to save herself from indolence after being so accustomed to rule and no longer able to fulfill her destined calling. Her conclusion was that the only solace for the afflicted was turning to God. Instead of withering in her imprisonment, the queen of Scots, in her solitary sufferings, turned her great courage inward, rediscovering in her spirit that vein of mysticism the devoted abbot from Inchmahone had long ago observed in her when she was barely five years old. Mary's spirit had also been prepared for her merciless treatment by witnessing her French grandmother's deep faith and daily reminder of her own death, as she passed her own coffin to attend daily Mass.

Elizabeth continued to vacillate between "fits of leniency and fits of vigor" toward her prisoner, who described herself to the English queen as the

poor, forsaken stranger princess who fled so trustingly for succor to her nearest kinswoman. I cannot but deplore my evil fortune, seeing you have been pleased not only to refuse me your presence, causing me to be declared unworthy of it by your nobles; but also suffered me to be torn in pieces by my rebels . . . not allowing me to have copies of their false accusations, or affording me any liberty to accuse them.

At one point, Elizabeth suggested to Mary: "If we were but two milkmaids with pails upon our arms, with no more depending upon the matter but my own life, and not the safety and welfare of the nation, I would most willingly pardon and remit this offense." However, she stated, "I am not so void of judgment as not to see mine own peril, nor yet so ignorant as not to know it were in nature foolish course to cherish a sword to cut mine own throat." As a safeguard, a Bond of Association was drawn up, with the queen of Scots in mind, that included acts of treason against the queen of England, justice against anyone including foreign monarchs crowned and uncrowned who would conspire against their queen.

After 1580, three major plots to rescue the queen of Scots

threatened the queen of England, as they allegedly involved her assassination. The last one, the Babington Plot, was the end for Mary. Mary never ceased to seek a way to her own freedom, but there is no indication that she ever wished or approved of a plan to murder Elizabeth. In the last years of her life, the last thing she wanted was to rule, she was so physically weak. In fact, she reacted with horror when the conspiracy was revealed.

Known for her fascination with cryptology, Mary delighted in invisible inks and all forms of secret writing. As she sought her freedom, she elevated cryptology to an art, urging her correspondents to reply on white taffeta with invisible ink, and to mark key words with a special symbol that she herself had devised.

Forgery, deciphering and surreptitious opening and closing of letters were at this time in history in a high state of perfection. One of the masters of this art was Walsingham, Elizabeth's closest advisor, an ambitious, cunning and heartless man, who ruined many innocent persons and fomented the insurrection of the Huguenots in France and wars in the Low Countries. Walsingham employed fifty-three secret agents and eighteen spies in all countries, including in the bedchambers of the papacy. He artfully wove plots in which many people got so entangled they could not escape. To his list of accomplishments, he, along with Burghley, another of Elizabeth's close advisors and a violent man, were "entrusted with the management and execution of the scheme which was to become the greatest tragedy in English history."[6]

With skill and audacity, the unscrupulous and unprincipled Walsingham set about the villainous destruction of the queen of Scots. His plot involved first setting her up with a new jailer, one who was completely immune to her charms. Sir Amyus Paulet, a staunch Puritan, was an avowed enemy of the queen of Scots. Paulet's first act was to take down Mary's cloth of state. To punish her, he then forbade any outside exercise, "for that heretofore under colour of giving alms and other extraordinary courses used by her, she hath won the hearts of the people . . ." Her alms were given in exchange for the villager's prayers, which Mary felt she desperately needed. Finally, Paulet cut her off from all outside correspondence.

This was essential to the plot. Walsingham knew Mary would seek a way to get letters out come hell or high water, and he devised a way for her to do so where he would be the recipient of all her correspondence.

When Babington, a good-looking young man with an enchanting way about him and considerable intelligence, approached Mary with a plan for her release, he told her he felt it was an honorable enterprise, "what they could and would perform or die." The legends that sprang up around the Babington Plot held an undercurrent of sexual excitement in the public's mind. Popular ballads sang of the bewitching of Babington's "senseless mind" by a woman old enough to be his mother. Even after years of captivity, Mary was seen as a terrible threat: a seductive witch who caused men to lose their will.

At this point, with the now-sadistic nature of her situation, Mary was ever more desperate to be free. Walsingham surreptitiously devised a way for Mary to send and receive correspondence through the brewer on his delivery days. Aided by his spies, Walsingham intercepted her correspondence, deciphered their code and then copied them over, introducing his own material, including the assassination plot, at last accomplishing Mary Stuart's destruction and the ruin of all involved. During a mock trial, under the duress of new and ghastly tortures, requested with bloodthirsty vengeance by Elizabeth, Babington and his companions confessed and then were executed in the most savage manner. While still alive, they were castrated, disemboweled, and quartered. Now in terror for her life, Elizabeth, as Walsingham had hoped, became resolved on Mary's execution.

DURING THIS SAME SUMMER of 1585, still unaware of the tangled web that would finally capture her, Mary received a horrible blow. The idea of an alliance with her son had been thoroughly undermined, as James had fallen prey to his own weaknesses and the treachery of others. Having for so long believed in his mother's guilt with regard to his father's death, it was easy to get him to believe she would conspire to have Elizabeth murdered. His own aspirations for the crown of England made it easy for him not to look too hard at the facts. His ambitious counselor, Gray, played everyone—James, Mary, Elizabeth—like a violin for his own ends. And so James betrayed his mother and declined the Bond of Association. Finally, the mother learned to her utter heartbreak that her son had actually signed a treaty of alliance with Elizabeth, and began to speak of James as her unfortunate and deluded son. Cut off from any news, Mary had no idea of the sudden and disastrous change in her fortunes.

Prone always to terrible fancies and now thoroughly deluded by her trusted advisor, the queen of England unleashed her full fury at the queen of Scots. "Under the colour of going a-hunting and taking the air, remove the queen to a house where the owner is removed, the servants left behind, and appoint standing watches in the town." Her long list of specific orders regarding the treatment of Mary Stuart struck terror even in the cold heart of Amyas Paulet. He was not to fail.

As she set out on a buck hunt so unexpectedly arranged by Paulet, the great joy of riding again in the open air that Mary felt can only be imagined. Fantasies of further leniency must have entered and delighted her mind. In her magnanimous mood and feeling compassion for his recent illness, she slowed her horse to allow Paulet to catch up when she noticed he was lagging behind. Suddenly, in the distance, she spotted riders racing toward their party. Were knights finally coming to her rescue?

As they approached, one dismounted—Elizabeth's emissary Thomas Gorges—dressed to the hilt in honor of the momentousness of the occasion. Paulet introduced him to the queen of Scots. "Madame," Gorges began, "the queen my mistress, finds it very strange that you, contrary to the pact and engagement made between you, should have conspired against her and her State, a thing which she could not have believed had she not seen proof of it with her own eyes and known for certain." Mary's vehement protests to the contrary fell on deaf ears. She was immediately separated from her servants, who were also accused and detained.

Meanwhile, her apartments at Chartley were being ransacked.

Carol Schaefer

Elizabeth wanted every bit of Mary's papers, "making care that all secret corners in the lodging be diligently searched," and the boxes containing them sealed. To accomplish this, Mary had to be taken to other living quarters. Paulet promised that the new residence was far superior. The queen of Scots would have none of it, and dismounting her horse, she sat down on the ground in the middle of the road, refusing to budge. Paulet threatened to throw her bodily into his carriage if she did not cooperate. Not until her servants pleaded with her to show herself "firm and composed within her royal heart" was she able to acquiesce. First, though, she insisted on kneeling under a tree to pray. As beautiful as Tixall of the ancient seat of Aston was, the distraught Mary could hardly have noticed as she arrived under heavy guard, with nothing but the gay riding clothes on her back. After a fortnight, during which she never left her chambers, Paulet informed her she would be returning to Chartley.

Beggars had gathered outside the gates of Tixall the morning of her departure, drawn by the legendary generosity of the Scottish queen. As the procession of one hundred and forty horses passed by, the poor people reached out for alms to the woman once considered a goddess. In tears, Mary turned toward them with tenderness. "Alas, good people, I have now nothing for you; all is taken from me. I am as much a beggar as you are yourselves."

14

A Poet's Tear

This evening the moon dreams more lazily;
As some fair woman, lost in cushions deep,
With gentle hand caresses listlessly
The contour of her breasts before she sleeps,
On velvet backs of avalanches soft
She often lies enraptured as she dies,
And gazes on white visions aloft
Which like a blossoming to heaven rise.
When sometimes on this globe, in indolence,
She lets a secret tear drop down, by chance,
A poet, set against oblivion,
Takes in his hand this pale and furtive tear,
This opal drop where rainbow hues appear,
And hides it in his breast far from the sun.

—*Charles Baudelaire*, Sorrows of the Moon

DURING HER FORTNIGHT at Tixall, Mary faced her imminent death
and decided to make it a triumph of her faith. If she were to die a
martyr for the Catholic Church, then her death and all her terrible
sufferings would have meaning and purpose. She may not be able to
end their persecution, but she could give them heart. Her only fear
now was the haunting possibility of a secret and solitary death by
poison, or a dagger in the dark, an unexplained fatal accident, a
death that barely made a ripple of a difference. Like a great light,
the deep inner strength from her resolve, that all now felt emanating from her, increased daily.

After being apart from their mistress a fortnight, tears of joy flowed as her devoted servants watched Mary approach Chartley. Swept back up into her little family, Mary learned a baby had been born to the wife of her secretary Curle, now imprisoned, and that Paulet had refused to allow a priest on the premises to perform a Baptism. Going straight to the mother's bedchamber, Mary rested the infant on her knee, took water out of the basin, and cast it upon the face of the child, now named Mary, saying, "Mary, I baptize thee in the name of the Father, the Son, and the Holy Ghost," as was allowed by the Church under extreme circumstances.

When she returned to her own chambers finally, Mary learned that all had indeed been taken from her. Soon after her discovery, Paulet, with the Staffordshire magistrate, forcibly entered Mary's room after she refused to see them, pleading illness. Her servants were sent away, trembling for their mistress, as they noticed the swords and daggers on the men now standing guard outside Mary's room. Her faithful physician Bourgoing managed to linger close by, as Mary was alone with the two dangerous men. Bourgoing had begun documenting in a journal all that was happening to Queen Mary.

During his ransacking of her quarters, Paulet had not found her money, and, threatening force, demanded she hand it over. Refusing, Mary said it was for her funeral expenses and to provide for her servants after she was gone. No match for his threats and climbing from her bed, the queen limped across the room barefooted, and retrieved the money from a secret compartment. "Two things cannot be taken from me," she declared, handing him the last of her money. "My royal blood and my Catholic religion, which I will keep until my death."

Paulet felt afflicted as his eyes fell on Mary's gold rosary, her prayer books and pictures in silk. To him all was "damnable wickedness and trash," and he hoped to see the root of Catholicism pulled up some day. He gave her back ten crowns of her own money and kept the rest. Leaving Mary's room, Paulet demanded that her servants be sent to various rooms, isolated from each other, never to see their mistress again. Only a few, the most essential to her household, were allowed to remain. No one knew what would happen next.

On the twenty-first of September, armed with pistols, Gorges and Stallenge, the usher of Parliament, informed Mary that she was to be moved once again. Evil was thick in the air. Her servants were locked in their rooms, prohibited by armed guards from looking out at their mistress one last time and offering her empathy.

No one was told the destination, only how long they could expect to be traveling each day. Two hundred horsemen, dressed in the livery of their masters and armed with swords and daggers, accompanied the carriage carrying the queen of Scots, too feeble now to ride on horseback. One hundred rode before her, one hundred behind. Mary sat with her back to the coachman, partly for comfort, partly so that he could hear her if she needed him, and partly to see what was going on behind her, wishing to see the blow coming should anyone wish to do her harm. Nearby was Paulet's coach with his wife and family, and his servants carrying harque-buses, pistols and lighted torches.

Gorges rode alongside the queen's carriage, and at one point said he had something to tell her from his mistress. Mary replied that she prayed God that his message was better than the last. He apologized that he was merely a servant, and Mary said she did not blame him. The first night, Gorges again said he wished to speak to her, but did not want to trouble her, since she would be tired from her journey. The next morning, as she prepared for the day's journey ahead, she sent for Gorges to ask what he wanted to tell her.

With strange and twisted logic, given Elizabeth's plans for her cousin, Gorges relayed that his queen was astounded and angry that a consecrated queen could ever consider laying her hands on another consecrated queen. As if to show how compassionate she really was, Elizabeth, despite her anger, considered sending Mary back to Scotland, but she feared her life would be in danger there. And, if she sent her to France, she worried Mary would have been thought a fool. Knowing full well that Walsingham was deceiving Elizabeth for his own purposes, Mary responded that, if his queen would only meet her, together they could both put an end to their enemies.

But Elizabeth chose to remain blind to the deception of those close to her, and instead became caught in Walsingham's web of intrigue and treachery. "For mine own life," she insisted, "I would not touch her." She did certainly believe plots on her own life thickened all around her. "Mary is the serpent that poisons me." Sifting through her dark and troubled thoughts she was overheard mumbling, "Aut fer, aut feri; ne feriare, feri." (Either suffer, or strike; not to be struck, strike.) If she spared Mary, she herself would be destroyed. So, as Mary journeyed to her last prison, Elizabeth was already arranging for her trial and demanding only one verdict.

Known for her insatiable spirit of vengeance and horrible temper, which she inherited from her Tudor relations and especially her father, King Henry VIII, it is remarkable that Elizabeth even appeared ambivalent. However, as a sophisticated and educated woman, Elizabeth had a great interest in the occult. She believed in the Doctrine of Correspondence, the teaching that everything created is connected by a powerful psychic force. Thus, to disturb one element in the balanced whole was to send shock waves through the rest of creation. "What goes around," in other words, "comes around." For her to authorize the taking of an anointed queen's life rent the web which enfolded all, and might well bring death back on her.

Fifty years before, when Elizabeth was only three years old, her own mother stood accused of treason by her father, just as her cousin Mary stood accused now by herself. Very much like Mary, Anne Bolyn had been "denounced as a wicked, unrepentant woman, faithless to her husband, an adulteress, who had plotted the death of her husband, lord and lawful sovereign." Was Elizabeth's blind spot to the truth of Mary's case caused by an unconscious need to understand and justify her own father's similar actions against her mother?

ON SUNDAY, SEPTEMBER 25, after four fatiguing days, the cortege reached its destination. Along the way each day, crowds sympathetic to the plight of Queen Mary had lined the route, and Paulet's coach had to be guarded against demonstrations. From a path called Perryho Lane, the ancient brooding towers of Fotheringhay loomed in the distance, and if Mary still carried a little hope in her heart, she could no longer. When she caught sight of the ancient castle she exclaimed, 'Perio! I perish!' Even in her distress she was unable to resist a play on words. The huge, grim, and forbidding castle with its long history of sorrows and crimes, set in a bleak and open landscape seventy miles north of London, had served as a state prison for over a century. This was the end of her tragic and weary pilgrimage.

Within the cold and fatal walls of the once-grand castle, Mary saw beautiful, empty rooms. Naturally she was upset then when she was shut up under heavy guard in chambers that were fairly ignoble; fear flared up again about the prospect of a secret assassination. Paulet began to systematically strip the queen of Scots of all her dignity. He took full control of every aspect of her life, including what she was allowed to eat. Without his permission, she could do nothing, although she did still try to stay on top of things. She even knew that her mare was about to foal.

When he took away her ceremonial rod that preceded her meals, Mary recalled from her extensive readings that the same thing was done to King Richard, who was "degraded from all honour and state, all signs of either, and then was suddenly put to death." When she confronted Paulet about such a similar demise for herself, he flew into a rage. She had offended his honor.

Her servants returned with information that the other rooms were to be used by arriving dignitaries. With this news in hand Mary knew she would have her wish: a public trial. Her physician, Bourgoing, noted that Mary's health made a sudden turn for the better upon learning of the trial, and her disposition became more cheerful than in a long time.

On October 1, Paulet relayed Elizabeth's message that she had sufficient proof against her. When Gorges had sped back to report the results of his conversation with Mary, Elizabeth reacted with shock. Now, Paulet relayed, Elizabeth demanded a full confession. Mary teased Paulet that his proposal sounded like how one would approach a child to elicit a confession. Devoid of humor, Paulet was silent, dumbstruck at her joke. With extraordinary dignity she gave him her final answer. "As a sinner, I am truly conscious of having often offended my Creator, and I beg Him to forgive me, but as Queen and Sovereign, I am aware of no fault or offense for which I have to render account to anyone here below. As therefore I could not offend, I do not wish for pardon; I do not seek, nor would I accept it from anyone living." Paulet wrote down her quotation word for word to send back to Elizabeth.

This statement was not said with arrogance. In a letter to the archbishop of Glasgow, she explained her understanding of what was meant by the Divine Right of Kings, what others may call imperiousness: ". . . God had called me by His Grace to this dignity, and I had been anointed and consecrated justly, and that from Him alone I held it, to Him alone should I render it with my soul." Thus she neither recognized Elizabeth as her superior nor anyone as her judge, her counsel or heretical assembly. "I should die queen in spite of them, and that they had no more power over me than robbers at the corner of a wood had over the most just prince or earthly judge." Mary was correct. As she was not a subject of the queen of England, to try her for treason was not even legal.

On October 11, the Lords of the Commission, fifty of them, began arriving. While some stayed at Fotheringhay, most stayed in the village and others were scattered about the countryside. Some of these men were outright enemies; some were forced to turn against her to save their estates. All were curious about her renowned beauty. Lord Shrewsbury was commanded to be on the commission, and when he begged illness he was threatened that noncompliance would mean all the rumors of his leniency toward the queen of Scots had been true. The only way he could avoid attending would be if he gave his guilty verdict ahead of time. Lord Burleigh, sent to persuade Shrewsbury, had his orders from his sovereign queen: "Upon the examination and trial of the cause, you shall by verdict find the said Queen guilty of the crime wherewith she standeth charged."

The lords gathered at the castle the next day, proceeding first to chapel for prayer and a sermon. Afterward, they met with Mary to persuade her to go to trial, thus guaranteeing its legality. Mary refused.

As an absolute Queen, I cannot submit to orders, nor can I submit to the laws of the land without injury to myself, the King my son and all other sovereign princes . . . For myself I do not recognize the laws of England nor do I know or understand them as I have often asserted. I am alone, without counsel, or anyone to speak on my behalf. My papers and notes have been taken from me, so that I am destitute of all aid, taken at a disadvantage, commanded to obey, and to reply to those who are well prepared and are my enemies, who only seek my ruin. I have made several offers to the Queen of England which have not been accepted, and now I hear that she has again entered into league with my son, thus separating mother from child.

James never seemed to realize his mother's life was in danger or that she could ever be brought to trial. His advisor Gray was very involved in keeping Elizabeth informed about James' feelings concerning his mother's predicament. Gray and Walsingham had managed to convince James that his mother was after his crown and a threat to Elizabeth, so that James believed prison, where she was not a real threat, was good for her. She could pray and serve God. Elizabeth believed that if she "did justice against the mother, she would be doing nothing else but advance the son." She warned James, "A woman who had not spared her husband, was not likely to spare her son."

Walsingham wrote to Gray advising him to tell the king not to mediate for his mother. The implication was his succession would be in severe jeopardy. After Babington, it further was implied, Elizabeth should be favored for showing clemency. As the trial commenced, Gray worried about his own position. His king would insist he advocate for his mother's life, when Gray's own well-being would be at stake should mother and son renew their correspondence. "Unpleasant secrets would be revealed," and mother and son would discover they had both been betrayed.

AS SHE CONTINUED TO argue against the trial, Mary claimed that if Catholic nations have come to her defense, she was not aware and could not be held responsible. Never had she heard of a plot against Elizabeth's life. With ostentatious ceremony, the lords finally told her she would be tried with or without her permission. The queen of Scots replied, "Look to your consciences and remember that the theater of the world is wider than the realm of England."

A guilty verdict and a private assassination were inevitable should she refuse. Mary knew that if she died without witnesses, she would be vulnerable to the blackening of her character. She needed witnesses to the travesty. She also needed her life to have meaning. On October 14, she relented, even though they refused her a public trial, and agreed to be tried on a single charge of plotting the assassination of the queen of England.

At 9:00 a.m. on Wednesday, October 15, the trial of the queen of Scots began. "With courage equal to her sorrows, Mary Stuart entered the large room with a guard of halberdiers, and faced her judges with all the dignity of her happier days." Her dress and mantle of flowing black velvet was set off by her traditional white headdress with widow's peak, covered by a long, gauzy white veil. Lack of exercise and severe rheumatism from the dark prisons of her last years caused her to walk with great difficulty, but with undiminished dignity. On either side to support her were Melville and Bourgoing. One of her ladies bore her train. The commissioners entered with ceremony and uncovered their heads before her. She saluted them with great majesty. When she saw that her seat of crimson velvet was placed beside the throne, outside the dais, and in a lower position, she exclaimed, "I am a queen by right of birth, and my place should be here, under the dais!" She did quickly recover her poise, however, preferring to keep her dignity in the face of their cruelty.

Only Burleigh was in charge. Neither the attorney general nor the queen sergeant took part, which was unprecedented in any other state trial of the period. Alone, with no counsel of her own, and allowed no papers or witnesses, Mary Stuart, queen of Scots, defended herself with great elegance and eloquence. At length, she explained she was only guilty of wanting her freedom, not of conspiring against Elizabeth's life.

> I am accused of having written to Christian princes in the interest of my freedom. I confess I have done so, and I should again. What human creature, O good God, would not do the same to escape from a captivity such as mine! You lay to my charge my letters to Babington. Well, it be so, I deny them not; only show me a single word in them about Elizabeth, and then I shall allow

your right to prosecute me. Do you not understand that princesses have secret correspondents, and it could not be otherwise?

Her accusers were unrelenting, and responded like raging madmen. "They went on and on against her, sometimes all together, sometimes one after the other, in order to frame the queen as guilty. But, the hotter they grew, the more courageous and constant were her replies."

That evening, Mary made notes to help her remember everything. "Her heart swelled with affliction; her spirits seemed to awaken and become stronger, which gave her strength to debate her cause." She then passed an anxious and sleepless night in preparation for her defense of their unremitting attacks. "Her day was begun in prayer, imploring for strength to defend her honor and her life." When she reentered the courtroom, she was very pale, but still firm and resolute.

Boldly, she told Burleigh that she believed Walsingham to be the mastermind behind the whole conspiracy, and went into great detail to prove her point, claiming he forged her ciphers and conspired against her son's life as well. Taken completely by surprise, Walsingham denied everything, defending himself as a faithful servant of his mistress and a gentleman. But, Mary replied, "Give no more heed to the words of those who slander me than I do to the statements of those who betray you. No value is to be attached to the testimony of those spies or agents whose words always give the lie to their hearts. Do not believe that I have been vain enough to wish that harm should be done to Elizabeth. No, I shall never seek her ruin at the cost of my honor, my conscience, or my salvation."

Mary told all assembled that she no longer wished to rule in the last few years of her life, should she be allowed them. "My advancing age and bodily weakness both prevent me from wishing to resume the reins of government. I have perhaps only two or three years to live in this world, and I do not aspire to any public position, especially when I consider the pain and desperance which meet those who wish to do right, and act with justice and dignity in the midst of so perverse a generation, and when a whole world is full of crimes and troubles.'"

The queen was certain there were those who sympathized with her, but did not dare speak up. To her mind, the lawyers and advocates seemed to "indulge in the technicalities used by the petty lawyers of the towns." Still, she "never lost heart, the more they warmed up to hinder her, the firmer she grew; her heart, her strength, her reason rose to the occasion."

On the third day, it was obvious that they had not intended a long trial, as many were booted and some dressed in riding habits, expecting to leave early. As the queen of Scots left the hall, she turned back to the commissioners with an extraordinary rebuke: "You have behaved severely with your charges, and have treated me pretty rudely for a person who is not learned in the laws of chicanery. May God pardon you and keep me from having much to do with you." They, "turning to each other, smiled, as also did her Majesty." How many realized they were witnessing true power?

A strange peace settled within the castle walls, as all awaited the sentencing. Bourgoing remarked he had not seen Mary so full of joy or so much at ease in over seven years. Even Paulet treated her with courtesy. She spoke only of light subjects. All traces of sadness were gone. As she prepared for her own noble death, she drew strength from books about heroic lives throughout history. In her heart she believed her Divine destiny, as the queen of Scots, demanded it of her. She still needed to feel she had brought some good into a troubled world.

On the twenty-third of November 1586, Mary was given her sentence of death by Buckhurst by order of Elizabeth, who, deflecting responsibility as it was her nature to do, felt "there was so much public opinion for this solution that she could not defy it." Two queens could not inhabit the same isle. Since Mary had been expecting it, she was not thrown by it. She was losing her life for the Catholic Church, and not for any designs on their sovereign's life. "She did not fear death and was quite resolute, and with a good heart would endure it." Her brilliant spirit held her in good stead and carried her through all her troubles.

Most of Europe denied the possibility that Elizabeth would

actually follow through on her threats. The French king, Henry III, expressed his grief over the unkind treatment of Elizabeth's illustrious prisoner, whom he felt was not under Elizabeth's jurisdiction. "This noble princess is so humbled and trodden underfoot that her greatest enemies outright to pity her . . ."

JAMES WAS BECOMING alarmed and wrote Elizabeth carefully worded letters, asking her to spare his mother's life. To his surprise, his own subjects were letting him know that they felt outrage that their Scottish queen might be put to death by a foreign sovereign. At this point, James appeared to be reacting with a kind of unreality. With the head of his mother already floating in the ethers of his country, what was the king of Scotland meant to do?

After the sentencing, Paulet's behavior toward Mary grew outrageous. Elizabeth had given him "carte blanche to treat Mary with every mark of cruelty."[1] On entering her chamber, he demanded that her dais be removed. Her servants refused to help with the dismantling, and Paulet had his men destroy it. In disrespect, Paulet put on his hat and sat down as he watched. He then demanded that her billiards table be taken away. "No further pastime was needed by a woman who was about to die." To further punish her lack of repentance, and to prevent her from being inflamed in her righteousness, Paulet refused her her priest, and then took away all of her servants. Her cloth of state was replaced with a crucifix.

Believing "even the wickedest of people would grant her last wishes," Mary again began to fear a secret assassination. Thus, when she wrote to a correspondent, "They are at present working on my hall, erecting the scaffold, I suppose wherein I am to perform the last act of this tragedy," the hammering and noise must have sounded like music to her ears.

While Elizabeth spoke of the weather, she blithely signed the warrant for Mary's death, and then sent out inquiries about the possibility of someone taking the responsibility for dealing the blow from her hands. It was Paulet in particular that she looked to. When her request was made known to him he was outraged, and wrote a letter back declining. Elizabeth lashed out in fury at his "daintiness." If no one could be found to murder the Scottish queen in secret, then the execution was under no circumstances to take place in public. Elizabeth forbade the subject be brought up again until the deed was done.

On February 3, the executioner was sequestered in an inn within Fotheringhay. Walsingham told Paulet, "His instrument is put in a trunk, and he passeth as a serving man." As if sensing his shadowy presence, Mary began to feel the blow was about to fall. All about her began to feel uneasy. On February 4, her physician Bourgoing requested permission to gather herbs in the adjoining gardens to alleviate some of the pain of Mary's rheumatism. At first Paulet refused the request, but then fearing she would become ill without them and spoil the execution, he relented. On February 7, when they saw Shrewsbury had arrived, there was no longer any doubt the time was close by.

That evening, those in charge of her execution requested an audience. Mary responded she was sick in bed, but she would see them if they gave her a little time. When the party entered her chambers, only Shrewsbury uncovered his head. Mary listened with calm and dignity as Shrewsbury apologized for what he was about to tell her. Her execution was set for the next morning at eight o'clock. Instead of shedding tears, she thanked him for "such welcome news. You will do me a great good in withdrawing me from this world, out of which I am very glad to go." Despite her royal position she felt, "All my life I have had only sorrow." Again she swore her innocence.

After the men left, she spent time in prayer with her women. She then divided up her money and put it in many little purses with slips of paper with each servant's name, setting aside some for the poor. With all she needed to do and so little time, supper was hurried. Bourgoing placed the dishes before her with one hand, wiping tears with the other. She ate little. At times she slipped into a "profound reverie, a sweet smile animated her countenance, as if she had received some fanciful tidings." After supper, she drank to the welfare of her servants, and they fell to their knees, "tears mixing with the wine," and begged her forgiveness for any transgressions, and she in turn begged for theirs, saying she wished she could have done more for them.

She wrote letters, distributed her meager possessions, and wrote her chaplain since she was not allowed a priest to hear her last confession and give her the last rites of the Church. She also wrote her will, which is preserved at the Scottish College in Paris, and still carries traces of her tears.

Her business done, she wanted to devote what little time she had to the things of eternity. In preparation for her last journey, she had her feet washed in imitation of Jesus. Finally, overcome with fatigue, she lay down without undressing. Her women, already dressed in mourning, watched and prayed around her. Every evening, it was Mary's custom to have some pages read on the life of a saint. This last night on earth, she chose the life of the good thief, who had died on the cross next to Jesus. "In truth he was a great sinner," Mary said. "but not so great as I have been. I wish to take him for my patron for the time that remains to me." Resting then for some hours, her eyes closed, hands crossed over her breast, she did not really sleep. Her women felt already Mary seemed to be communing with the angels. The sound of constant hammering and the tramping of the soldiers' boots never ceased the whole night.

AT DAWN, February 8, 1587, on what was to be a beautiful, sunny day, Mary arose and dressed, and went to the antechamber, which was arranged as an oratory, to pray. At one point, Bourgoing noticed she was becoming faint and offered her a little bread and wine. At nine o'clock there came a knock on her door. She kept the door locked until she finished her prayers. Not trusting her, the sheriff was ready to storm the door, when a servant opened it on the second knock. The sheriff entered alone. Silent from surprise and perhaps emotion at the sight of her kneeling so rapt in prayer, he finally murmured, "Madame, the lords have sent me to you."

"Yes, let us go," she said quietly, composed.

At the threshold, Bourgoing stated that neither he nor her attendants would offer their arm to lead her to her death, and so two of Paulet's soldiers assisted her. At the entrance to the Great Hall, all her attendants were stopped from entering. Against their protests that their queen had never been left unattended, they were forced back into the queen's apartments by orders of Elizabeth, who wished for Mary to die alone. The wails from their grief were heart-breaking. As they were pulled away from their mistress, they kissed her hands and the hem of her dress. Mary took the gold cross and gold embroidered handkerchief they were holding, and entered the hall alone.

At the foot of the steps, she discovered her old friend and sup-porter, James Melville, who knelt before her and grieved that he must witness such a spectacle after not having seen her for so long. He could not bear to think of her having to die alone. "Oh Madam," he cried. "It will be the sorrowfullest message that I ever carried when I shall report that my Queen and dear mistress is dead." Wip-ing away her own tears, Mary gently said to him:

> You ought to rejoice and not weep for that the end of Mary Stuart's troubles is now done. Thou knowest, Melville, that all this world is but vanity and full of troubles and sorrows. Carry this message from me and tell my friends that I died a woman true to my reli-gion, and like a true Scottish woman and a true French woman.

She asked that Melville go to her son, and tell him her dearest wish had always been to see England and Scotland united, and to trust she had done nothing to jeopardize her country. "Tell him to keep me in memory, and report to him faithfully what you shalt have seen of his mother's last moments. Take him my blessing." She made the sign of the cross, as if personally sending the blessing to her son. Bidding Melville adieu, she had to again fight tears. It was the first time she had ever used the familiar "thou" with anyone.

Turning to the lords, she begged them to allow her servants be with her. They said they were worried for their cries and that they might dip their handkerchiefs in her blood. She swore they would keep silent. "Do you then forget that I am cousin to your queen, that I am of the blood royal of Henry VII, that I am Queen Dowager of France, and anointed Queen of Scotland!" They relented, but only two of the women were allowed—Jane Kennedy and Elizabeth Curle.

Melville, Bourgoing and three others were also allowed in. Surprised to be let back down into the hall, they thought their queen must have already died. When they first saw her they cried out. Mary held up her hand, willing them to forbear so that she may have them with her. The lords witnessed a "wonderful show of subjection and loyal obedience. For though their breasts were seen to rise and swell as if their wounded hearts would burst asunder, yet did they (to their double grief) forbear outward plaints to accomplish her pleasure."[2]

As musicians played a dirge commonly reserved for witches, the procession moved on and entered the Great Hall draped all in black. The majestic queen of Scots followed the sheriff and the lords. Melville carried her train. Three hundred spectators awaited her. Thousands thronged outside. Their shouts must have reached inside the hall to Mary.

At first sight of the scaffold, she raised her ivory cross over her head and advanced with great dignity. As the queen accepted Paulet's arm for assistance with the two short steps up to the twelve-foot square platform, she said to him, "Thank you for your courtesy, Sir Amyus. This will be the last trouble I shall give you, and the most agreeable service you have ever rendered me."

The block, covered with black, was placed near the great gothic fireplace. Nearby stood the executioner and his assistant, both dressed in long black velvet gowns, with white aprons and black masks. The executioner held a large ax mounted on a short handle, such as used for chopping wood. Around the scaffold was a guard of halberdiers. With majesty, Mary Stuart took her seat on the black-serge covered stool. The Royal Commission for Execution was read, and after commanding them to do their duty, she addressed the hall with a joyousness that made her appear more beautiful than ever.

When the dean of Peterborough began to exhort her to prayer, she asked him kindly to leave her presence. When he kept up his harangue, she asked him again saying he would gain nothing. Shocked at the dean's behavior, Shrewsbury asked him to be silent. All in the hall prayed loudly for God to grant Mary repentance, and to bless Queen Elizabeth, grant her a long life and victory over her enemies, and triumph of the Protestant religion. Mary prayed in

English, expressing the deep passion of her soul. Silence filled the hall when their prayers were finished. Asked one more time to confess, Mary replied she had said all she needed to say.

Seeing it was time, Mary arose without being asked. The masked executioner approached to remove her dress. Mary gently moved him to the side and smiled, "Let me do this; I understand this business better than you. I never had such a groom of the chamber." When she took her gold cross from her neck, the executioner roughly seized it. When Mary protested that it was for her servant Jane, and that he would be compensated, he said it was his right, and stuck it in his shoe. As her women helped her undress, she joked to the spectators, "I never have had such grooms before to make me unready, nor ever took off my clothes before such company." The crowd gasped, as suddenly Mary stood stripped to her red petticoat.

As she embraced her servants, she bid them "Adieu for the last time. Adieu, au revoir!" "Please," she asked one last time. "Remember me to my sweet son." Jane Kennedy covered her eyes with the beautiful handkerchief and stepped away. Begging her forgiveness, which was traditional, the executioner fell to his knees before her. She forgave him with all of her heart, as she had already forgiven everyone, even, and perhaps especially, Elizabeth.

Still seated and unbound, she stretched out her neck, believing she was to be beheaded by sword as was traditional in France for royalty. Seeing her misunderstanding, the executioner assisted her to her feet and escorted her to the block, where he helped her kneel down. The hall was deadly silent. When he tried to bind her with cords, she pushed them aside. Still thinking she would be dying by the sword, she knelt upright. But they made her bend, with her head on the low block, only a few inches high from the ground. Mary could be heard saying in Latin, "Into Thy hands O Lord I commend my spirit."

Lord Shrewsbury, her jailer for fourteen years, raised his wand to give the fatal signal. As the ax was poised over the executioner's head, he was stopped by his assistant. To enable herself to breath, the queen had placed her hands under her chin. The assistant moved them and held them behind her back. The hall was held in profound suspense. Weakened by the intense emotions, the executioner's first blow was not fatal. Someone thought they heard Mary say, "Sweet Jesus!" The second blow was fatal, but it took one more to completely sever her head. Mary Stuart was forty-four years old. The last entry in her physician Bourgoing's journal read: "And immediately her spirit passed away, and the Queen of Scots was delivered from all her cares."

When her head toppled off the block Mary's body began moving. Terror swept through the crowd. When the executioner held up her head for all to see, it slipped from her wig and fell to the floor. Mary's own hair had turned white, and she was nearly bald from her long imprisonment. Without her great spirit to animate it, the enchanting face of legendary beauty was suddenly unrecognizable, withered now like a crone's. The lips remained moving, as if still praying, for the next fifteen minutes.

Reaching under the queen's skirt to claim her garter, which was his prerogative, the executioner's heart stopped. Mary's little Skye terrier, Geddon, devoted companion during her last years in prison, came out from hiding under her voluminous skirts and refused to leave his dead mistress. He lay down protectively in the pool of blood between her head and her body.

The gates of the castle remained locked. No one was to leave until a messenger was dispatched to Elizabeth with a letter and certificate of execution. Everyone was commanded to leave the hall immediately, except the sheriff and his men.

Geddon remained trembling close by his mistress' body as the executioner picked up her head, placed it on a dish, and standing by the window, raised it up and showed it to the crowd in the courtyard outside. "This he did three times," not comprehending what he was evoking. Ancient Celts believed the soul was housed in the skull—and that belief, long forgotten, was the original reason for the practice of beheading. Framed by the opened window and raising her head up to the throngs outside, in much the same gesture a priest offers the Eucharist, the executioner offered up Mary's soul to the world's dreamlife.

It was not until her son, James, finally claimed his mother that her magnificent spirit could truly rest in peace.

Epilogue

She is buried with honour, as dead rose leaves are preserved,
whence the liquor that makes the kingdom sweet hath been distilled.

—Earl of Northhampton to King James I & VI

SOMEONE PRIED LITTLE GEDDON away from Mary's body and washed him over and over, so that no blood remained. Anything that had even a drop of the queen of Scots blood was burned or washed clean. There were to be no holy relics made from her martyrdom. Her body was carried up to the great chamber, laid out on her own billiard table, and hastily rolled in cloth torn from it, awaiting the surgeons to embalm her. Her women, banished from attending to her, watched through the keyhole of their adjoining room, kneeling and praying by the door. When Paulet discovered them, he had the keyhole stopped up. By four in the afternoon, her body was stripped, embalmed, wrapped in a waxed winding sheet, placed in a heavy leaded coffin, and sealed shut.

For six long months, the body of Mary Stuart was to remain neglected and forgotten within the ancient walls of Fotheringhay.

Geddon refused to eat and soon died.

Elizabeth dressed in mourning weeds and shed copious and histrionic public tears. Still she asked that bells be rung throughout the country for the next twenty-four hours without ceasing. The news was received with fanatic joy by her subjects, who considered

Elizabeth the queen of the common people. During her reign, England had grown from obscurity to a flourishing and important nation. Finally disgusted with her lavish show of grief, Cecil harshly warned Elizabeth to drop the act. No one in Europe would buy it, and many may become seriously offended. Davison was thrown into prison for a short while for his audacity in implementing the warrant, which she herself signed.

The whole nation of France grieved their dowager queen. On March 12, the black-draped Notre Dame Cathedral, site of her solemn Requiem Mass, was filled with mourners who only remembered the wondrous goddess who once walked down the majestic aisle during her magnificent wedding ceremony. The archbishop of Bourges spoke with befitting and extraordinary eloquence of the tragedy they all comprehended more than anyone else in the world ever would:

Many of us saw in the place where we are now assembled to deplore her, this Queen on the day of her bridal, arrayed in her regal trappings, so covered in jewels that the sun himself shone not more brightly, so beautiful, so charming withal as never woman was. These walls were then hung with cloth of gold and precious tapestry; every space was filled with thrones and seats, crowded with princes and princesses, who came from all parts to share in the rejoicing. The palace was overflowing with magnificence, splendid fetes and masques; the streets with jousts and tourneys. In short it seemed as if our age had succeeded that day in surpassing the pomp of all past centuries combined. A little time has flowed on and it is all vanished like a cloud. Who would have believed that such a change could have befallen her who appeared then so triumphant, and that we should have seen her a prisoner who had restored prisoners to liberty; in poverty who was accustomed to give so liberally to others; treated with contumely by those on whom she had conferred honours; and finally, the axe of a base executioner mangling the form of her who was doubly a queen; that form which honoured the nuptial bed of a sovereign of France, falling dishonored on a scaffold, and that beauty which had been one of the wonders of the world, faded in a dreary prison, and at last effaced by a piteous death. This place, where she was surrounded with splendour, is now hung with black for her. Instead of nuptial torches we have funeral tapers; in the place of songs of joy, we have sighs and groans; for clarions and hautboys, the tolling of the sad and dismal bell. Oh God, what a change! Oh vanity of human greatness, shall we never be convinced of your deceitfulness . . .[1]

James did not learn of his mother's death until Roger Ashton brought the news around February 14. The accounts of his reaction are conflicting and range from indolence, to joy, to shock and grief. There was widespread indignation on the part of the Scottish people, which James was afraid to ignite or control. Some of the lords urged him to go to war, and there were rumors of an invasion.

Tales of her heroic death began to leak out, despite all the precautions by the English. Her courage became as legendary as her beauty.

Catholics began calling for better treatment of her remains. By torchlight, on Sunday night at ten o'clock, July 30, 1587, the body of Mary Stuart was transported from Fotheringhay by a royal coach drawn by four horses covered in black velvet. The late hour was chosen to avoid demonstrations. Dressed in black at the government's expense the procession was lead by 100 widows. Between one and two in the morning, the 900-pound casket was interred in the nave of Peterborough Cathedral, without bells or chanting. The queen of Scots' tomb was opposite those of Catherine of Aragon and Scarlet the gravedigger. The coffin was lowered and the grave covered with brick, leaving a small opening. An elaborate ceremony, meaning little to anyone except her servants who stood by, the only ones weeping, was held the next day.

The king spoke of his mother as dead while alive, and, as living when she was dead. Mary's servants were not released from Fotheringhay until October, and it took Jane Kennedy almost a year to fulfill her mistress' wish to give James an accurate accounting of his mother's death. James talked to Jane for two hours, and was "very sad and pensive all that day, and would not supp that night." Jane told James how the queen was "martyred and mangled" by the executioner, describing the scene with dramatic words and gestures. The Venetian diplomat observed after James' ascension to the English throne that, haunted by her memory, he never "let a day pass without lamenting that his mother's head fell, at the third stroke, by a villainous deed, till those who even by relationship are stained with that blood grow fearful . . . lest their end be a bloody one." Pictures of Elizabeth were hidden, and those of his mother put up instead. No longer surrounded by her enemies and fighting for the crown of England, he was able to say, "She suffered for no cause except her religion." "For fifteen years, I was among them, but not of them: how they treated that poor lady, my mother, is only too well known." Later in life, in a book to his son, the *Basilikon Doron*, he warned Prince Henry against taking the part of his parents' enemies. "It is a thing monstrous to see a man love the childe and hate the parents . . . and for conclusion of this point, I may also allege my own experience."

Sixteen years after her death, James commissioned his master mason, Cornelius Lure, to create a monument to, as appeared on his final bill, his majesty's dearest mother. Escorted on the autumn night of October 8, 1612, by torchlight, Mary Stuart was royally and sumptuously reinterred on the south side of the Henry VII chapel in Westminster Abbey in a majestic white alabaster monument, just feet away from her cousin Elizabeth, so much closer in death than they ever came in life. "All the bitterness and tragedy, all the passions roused by their deadly rivalry, transmuted by time into dust and marble." [2] Just as Mary would have it.

In the Spring of 1856, three hundred years after her death, American novelist Nathaniel Hawthorne made a journey to the home of Sir Walter Scot, where he saw a painting of the head of Mary Queen of Scots lying in a dish and was deeply moved. "Her expression of quiet after much pain and trouble was very beautiful, very sweet and sad; and it affected me strongly with the horror and strangeness of such a head being separated from its body."

In 1867, a search for the body of James I, found to be in the tomb of his great grandfather Henry VII, uncovered more than a little irony and justice. Elizabeth was found buried alongside her half sister Mary Tudor, their bloodlines extinguished. Mary Stuart's tomb, it was discovered, was heaped with coffins of young people and babies—all her descendants. Through her son James, who became a great king of both England and Scotland, fulfilling her wish of uniting both countries, all rulers down to the present Elizabeth II are direct descendants. A portion of her magic certainly could be imagined through Princess Diana, a descendent of the queen of Scots. The tremendous outpouring of grief for Princess Diana may have also been tapping into the unexpressed and ancient grief for Mary Stuart, Queen of Scots, still lingering in our collective dream life.

Four hundred and fourteen years after her tragic end, there are still shrines to Mary Queen of Scots. Linlithgow, the place of her birth, is one such shrine for the devoted. Tourists make pilgrimages to the palaces where she lived and hire boats to transport themselves to Lochleven Island, her first place of imprisonment. Her tomb in Westminster Abbey is held sacred by many. Some claim miracles happen there. Wearing clothes of Mary's time, Scottish women hold seances on the anniversary of her death. Literature and art reflect a nation's dream work. Hundreds and hundreds of biographies have been written over the centuries and through the generations, reflecting as much about each era as the complicated and mysterious woman they were writing about. Artists still paint her, and over a hundred plays and other works of fiction and poetry have been inspired by this captivating woman, who herself was held captive for nearly half her life.

Was Mary Queen of Scots, this highly gifted and legendary beauty, an ill-starred princess? Or did we create her mythology to help us remember another much more ancient tragedy? Was she saint and martyr as so many believed, or simply a murderess and adulteress as so many others thought? It is now the new millennium, and still we have not yet solved the mystery of this woman's enchantment, or the tears she still evokes from so many.

ACKNOWLEDGEMENTS

In the darkness of an early spring evening in London in 1977, I visited Westminster Abbey alone. Only a handful of tourists were there. Few people knew it was open that night. As I wandered, with the great cathedral all to myself, everything felt strangely familiar. Now, as I look back and remember that night, there was a feeling of my footsteps being guided. When I discovered the majestic monument of Mary Queen of Scots, something came over me. I had not known enough about her to even know she was buried there. Touching her tomb, startling tears came to my eyes. Were these tears from deep within me, or were they hers? It was as if Mary Stuart, Queen of Scots, had, in some strange way, reached through time and touched me at my core.

Ten years after my visit to Mary's tomb, my father researched our roots. We suspected we were of Scotch/Irish descent, but we had no idea that our roots went through all of Scottish history, and that we were direct descendants of four Scottish kings, including Robert the Bruce. A connection to Mary Queen of Scots was made. These were ancestors we shared, and many more of ours were very much involved in her life. I wonder, too, if over the years Mary reached through time to me because we shared a similar grief? Both of us lost our firstborn sons.

I am grateful to Crossroad Publishing and my editor, Barbara Leah Ellis, for giving me the opportunity to immerse myself in the life of this extraordinary woman and attempt to solve, after all these years, the mystery of the surprising emotions I felt visiting Mary's tomb.

When good friends, playwright Arthur Giron and his wife

Marie Luce Giron, revealed they, too, had a similar experience when accidentally coming upon her tomb, they confirmed what I began to suspect, that I had fallen under the spell of the queen of Scots' legendary enchantment. Their validation confirmed there just might be a vein of Mary's story that I was sensing and feeling compelled to explore, but had no words for.

As I did my research, mostly in the exquisite Rose Reading Room at the New York Public Library that amazingly holds well over three hundred books about Mary and allowed me to imagine the opulence in which she grew up, I discovered Jayne Elizabeth Lewis' book *Romance and Nation*. Her brilliant interpretation of Mary's life provided an explanation for my intuitive promptings.

I am grateful to all the wonderful authors who spoke to me from over the centuries and gave me a fantastic glimpse at how humanity changes over time, as each interpreted Mary's life in the language of their times and through their eyes. I am especially grateful to Antonia Fraser, for the exhaustive research and elegant writing in her biography, *Mary Queen of Scots*. Chairman of the Marie Stuart Society of Edinburgh, Scotland, Ronald Morrison was also a great and helpful resource. The one to guide me to just the right books to explore Mary's vein of mysticism, Harlan Margold, with his extensive knowledge of historical figures, was an enormous source of support. I am very grateful to him.

I thank my Scottish friend Carol Solloway for keeping the land of my ancestors alive in my mind and heart. I am particularly grateful to Jane Guttman and Lynn Franklyn, both authors and good friends; Steve Loring, screenwriter of *The Other Mother* and mentor; and, Paula Mickey and Susan Deikman for their invaluable support. And always I will be grateful to Lee Sankowich for believing in me a long time ago; to Art Toulinoff for being there for me on every level throughout this project; to Bob Kirby for being the best brother anyone could wish for; and, especially for the love and support of my terrific sons and their great wives: Jack and Anna Ryan, Brett and Jessica Schaefer, and Kip and DeAnna Schaefer; and, finally, for my beloved grandchildren: Dylan, Mia, Asia and Tess Ryan, and Cole Schaefer.

CHRONOLOGY

1538 May: Marriage of James V of Scotland to Marie de Guise-Lorraine

1542 Dec. 8: Birth of Mary Stuart at Linlithgow
Dec. 14: Death of James V of Scotland
       Mary succeeds her father to the throne

1543 Sept. 9: Coronation of Mary Stuart at Stirling Castle; her
       mother becomes regent, aided by Cardinal Beaton

1544 Henry VIII of England's "Rough Wooing" of queen of
Scots for his son Edward VI

1546 War between England and Scotland

1546 May 29: Assassination of Cardinal Beaton, primate of
Scotland

1547 Jan. 28: Death of Henry VIII; ascension of Edward VI
Mar. 31: Death of Francis I, king of France; ascension of
Henry II
Sept. 10: English victory over Scots at Pinkie
       Mary Stuart is sent to Inchmahone Priory for safety

1548 Jul. 7: Treaty of Haddington signed between French and
       Scots; Mary is betrothed to Francois, dauphin of France
Aug. 7: Mary leaves Scotland for safety of France
Aug. 13: Mary arrives in France to be educated at St.
       Germaine-en-Laye with the children of Henri II and
       Catherine de' Medici

1550 Mar.: Peace between England and France negotiated

1551 June: Peace between England and Scotland negotiated

1553 Jul. 6: Death of Edward VI of England; ascension of Mary
      Tudor

1558 Apr. 11: Mary and Francois officially betrothed in Great
      Hall of Louvres Palace in Paris
      Apr. 24: Mary and Francois married at Notre Dame
      Cathedral in Paris; secret marriage contract signed, giv-
      ing Scotland to France should Mary die

      Nov. 17: Mary Tudor dies; ascension of Elizabeth Tudor;
      Henri II promotes Mary as queen, of England, his son as
      king

1559 Apr.: England, France and Spain sign Treaty of Cateau-
      Cambresis
      Jul.: Henri II dies in a jousting tournament; Francois
      ascends as king, Mary as queen, of France; supremacy of
      the Guises

1560 Feb.: Elizabeth I signs Treaty of Berwick, promising to sup-
      port Protestant Scots in rebellion against Marie de Guise
      Mar.: Siege of Leith against Marie de Guise; she retreats to
      Edinburgh Castle
      June 11: Marie de Guise dies of dropsy
      July 6: Treaty of Edinburgh signed agreeing to English and
      French withdrawal from Scotland, providing Elizabeth I
      is recognized as rightful queen of England
      Dec. 5: Francois dies of ear infection; Charles IX ascends
      with mother, Catherine de Medici as regent

1561 Aug. 14: Mary departs from Calais, France

      Aug. 19: Mary sails into Leith Harbor in Scotland at 9:00 a.m.

1565 Jul. 29: Mary marries Lord Darnley
      August 26: Mary sets out to confront brother James, and
      rebel lords in Chaseabout Raid

1566 Mar. 9: David Riccio savagely stabbed to death in Mary's
      presence
      June 19: Mary gives birth to Prince James, who will become
      James VI of Scotland and James I of England
      Dec. 17: Baptism of Prince James at Stirling

1567 Feb. 10: Darnley is murdered at Kirk o' Field
      Apr. 19: Bothwell gets 29 lords to sign Ainslee Bond, agree-
      ing to support his claims to wed Mary

Apr. 24: Mary visits son for last time; Bothwell abducts her and takes her to his castle at Dunbar

May 7: Bothwell obtains divorce from his wife, Lady Jean Gordon

May 15: Mary and Bothwell marry in Protestant service

June 15: Mary surrenders at Carberry Hill; betrayed, is taken prisoner

June 17: Lords Lindsay and Ruthven imprison Mary in Lochleven Castle

June 24: Mary miscarries twins; is forced to abdicate in favor of her son; her brother, James becomes regent

June 27: Bothwell attempts to escape; is thrown into Danish prison

July 29: Mary's son, thirteen months old, is crowned King James VI of Scotland

1568 May 2: Mary escapes from Lochleven

May 13: Mary defeated at the Battle of Langside

May 16: In disguise, Mary crosses Solway River; lands at Workington, on coast of Cumberland, England

May 18: Mary escorted to Carlysle Castle; gradual imprisonment begins

June 8: Elizabeth declares she cannot receive Mary until her name is cleared of Darnley's death

Oct.: "Casket Letters" produced: although copies and clearly forged, they are accepted as proof of Mary's guilt; Mary is given no opportunity to defend herself

1569 Feb. 3: Mary imprisoned in Tutbury Castle

Jul.: Elizabeth discovers Mary's plan to marry duke of Norfolk; throws him in Tower

1572 Jan.: Norfolk executed for involvement in Ridolphi Plot to free Mary

1578 Apr.: Bothwell dies in Danish prison

1581 English government makes it high treason to reconcile to Catholic Faith

1583 Nov.: Throckmorton Plot

1585 Jan.: Amyas Paulet becomes Mary's new jailer

Mar.: Mary's son repudiates association for joint rulership with Mary

Apr.: Bond of Association passed making Mary responsible

for any plot against Elizabeth

1586   Jan.: Walsingham begins plan to ensnare Mary in
       Babington Plot
       Aug.: Babington sent to Tower and confesses
       Aug. 11: Mary Queen of Scots is arrested
       Sept. 25: Mary taken to Fotheringhay
       Oct. 15: Three-day trial on charge of plotting Elizabeth's
       assassination begins; Mary is given no counsel and
       allowed no notes as she defends herself
       Nov. 19: Mary learns of her sentence of execution; refuses
       to confess

1587   Feb. 1: Elizabeth signs Mary's death warrant
       Feb. 7: Mary learns in evening she will be executed next
       morning
       Feb. 8: Mary beheaded in Great Hall of Fotheringhay
       July 29: Her body is buried at Peterborough Cathedral

1612   Oct. 11: Mary's body reinterred at Westminster Abbey in
       monument built by her son, James I of England

NOTES

CHAPTER 1: IN MY END IS MY BEGINNING

1. Hon. Mrs. Maxwell-Scott of Abbotsford, *The Tragedy of Fotheringhay: Found in the Journal of D. Bourgoing, Physician to Mary Queen of Scots*, p. 199.

CHAPTER 3: THE SCOTS' BETRAYAL

1. Antonia Fraser, *Mary Queen of Scots*, p. 28.

CHAPTER 4: HER SIMPLE GLANCE

1. Martin Hume, *The Love Affairs of Mary Queen of Scots: A Political History*, p. 58.

2 J. J. Foster, *The Stuarts: Being Illustrations of the Personal History of the Family, Vol. 1*, p. 17.

3. Hume, p. 42.

CHAPTER 5: THE FRENCH COURT

1. J. J. Foster, *The Stuarts: Being Illustrations of the Personal History of the Family, Vol. 1*, p. 15.

2. Alison Plowden, *The Young Elizabeth: The First Twenty-five Years of Elizabeth I*, p. 38.

CHAPTER 6: QUEEN OF FRANCE

1. J. J. Foster, *The Stuarts: Being Illustrations of the Personal History of the Family, Vol. 1*, p. 87.

2. Alison Plowden, *The Young Elizabeth: The First Twenty-five Years of Elizabeth I*, p. 212.

3. Carmen Boulter, *Angels and Archetypes: An Evolutionary Map of Feminine Consciousness*, p. 1.

4. Michael and Leigh Richard Baigent, *The Temple and the Lodge*, p. 107.

CHAPTER 7: QUEEN DOWAGER

1. Bernard Clarke Weber, *The Youth of Mary Stuart, Queen of Scots*, p. 51.

2. Martin Hume, *The Love Affairs of Mary Queen of Scots: A Political History*, p. 95.

3. Carolly Erickson, *The First Elizabeth*, p. 232.

4. J. J. Foster, *The Stuarts: Being Illustrations of the Personal History of the Family, Vol. 1*, p. 28.

CHAPTER 8: ADIEU FRANCE!

1. Bernard Clarke Weber, *The Youth of Mary Stuart, Queen of Scots*, p. 95.

2. J. J. Foster, *The Stuarts: Being Illustrations of the Personal History of the Family, Vol. 1*, p. 35.

3. Martin Hume, *The Love Affairs of Mary Queen of Scots: A Political History*, p. 98.

4. Foster, p. 88.

5. Ibid., p. 24.

6. Jayne Elizabeth Lewis, *Mary Queen of Scots: Romance and Nation*, p. 4.

7. Suzanne Schaup, *Sophia: Aspects of the Divine Feminine Past and Present*, p. 36.

CHAPTER 9: HER SCOTTISH COURT

1. Antonia Fraser, *Mary Queen of Scots*, p. 162.

2. J. J. Foster, *The Stuarts: Being Illustrations of the Personal History of the Family, Vol. 1*, p. 37.

3. Carolly Erickson, *The First Elizabeth*, p. 7.

4. Francois Laroque, *The Age of Shakespeare*, p. 3.

5. Martin Hume, *The Love Affairs of Mary Queen of Scots: A Political History*, p. 167.

CHAPTER 10: A HUSBAND

1. Alison Plowden, *The Young Elizabeth: The First Twenty-five*

Years of Elizabeth I, p. 94.

2. Martin Hume, *The Love Affairs of Mary Queen of Scots: A Political History*, p. 96.

3. Ibid., p. 277.

4. Plowden, p. 103.

CHAPTER 11: THE HALE BIRLIN' WORLD

1. Antonia Fraser, *Mary Queen of Scots*, p. 310.

CHAPTER 12: ESCAPE

1. J. J. Foster, *The Stuarts: Being Illustrations of the Personal History of the Family, Vol. 1*, p. 54.

CHAPTER 13: CAPTIVE QUEEN

1. Alison Plowden, *Two Queens in One Isle: The Deadly Relationship of Elizabeth I and Mary Queen of Scots*, p. 145.

2. Antonia Fraser, *Mary Queen of Scots*, p. 375.

3. Robert S. Rait and Annie I. Cameron, *King James's Secret: Negotiations Between Elizabeth I and James VI Relating to the Execution of Mary Queen of Scots, From the Warrender Papers*, p. 8.

4. Carolly Erickson, *The First Elizabeth*, p. 360.

5. Plowden, p. 184.

6. Samuel Cowan, *Last Days of Mary Stuart and the Journal of Bourgoing Her Physician*, p. 38.

CHAPTER 14: A POET'S TEAR

1. Samuel Cowan, *Last Days of Mary Stuart and the Journal of Bourgoing Her Physician*, p. 17.

2. Hon. Mrs. Maxwell-Scott of Abbotsford, *The Tragedy of Fotheringhay: Found in the Journal of D. Bourgoing, Physician to Mary Queen of Scots*, p. 210.

EPILOGUE

1. Antonia Fraser, *Mary Queen of Scots*, pp. 543–544.

2. Alison Plowden, *Two Queens in One Isle: The Deadly Relationship of Elizabeth I and Mary Queen of Scots*, p. 2.

BIBLIOGRAPHY

Baigent, Michael and Leigh, Richard. *The Temple and the Lodge*, New York: Arcade Publishing, 1989.

Bernstein, Henrietta. *Arc of the Covenant, Holy Grail*, Marina del Rey, CA: Devorss Publications, 1998.

Bierlein, J.F. *Living Myths: How Myth Gives Meaning to Human Experience*, New York: Ballantine Wellspring, The Ballantine Publishing Group, 1999.

Boulter, Carmen. *Angles and Archetypes: An Evolutionary Map of Feminine Consciousness*, Rapid City, SD: Sway-Raven Co., 1997.

Campbell, Joseph. *Transformations of Myth Through Time*, New York: HarperPerennial, 1999.

Cowan, Samuel. *Last Days of Mary Stuart and the Journal of Bougoing Her Physician*, London: Eveleigh Nash Publishers, 1907.

Erickson, Carolly. *The First Elizabeth*, New York: St. Martin's Griffin, 1983.

Foster, J.J. *The Stuarts: Being Illustrations of the Personal History of the Family*, Vol. 1, London: Dickensons, 1902.

Fraser, Antonia. *Mary Queen of Scots*, New York: Delta Publishing of Bantam Doubleday Dell Publishing Group, Inc., 1993.

George, Margaret. *Mary Queen of Scotland and the Isles*, New York: St. Martins Press, 1992.

Hume, Martin. *The Love Affairs of Mary Queen of Scots: A Political History*, London: Eveleigh Nash Publishers, 1903.

Laroque, Francois. *The Age of Shakespeare*, London: Harry N. Abrams, Inc., Publishers, 1991.

Lewis, Jayne Elizabeth. *Mary Queen of Scots: Romance and Nation,* London and New York: Routledge, 1998.

Lochead, Liz. *Mary Queen of Scots Got Her Head Chopped Off,* Great Britain: Penguin Books, 1989.

Maxwell-Scott, Hon. Mrs. of Abbotsford. *The Tragedy of Fotheringhay: Found in the Journal of D. Bourgoing, Physician to Mary Queen of Scots, and Unpublished Documents,* London: Adam & Charles Black, 1895.

Michael of Albany, *HRH Prince. The Forgotten Monarchy of Scotland: The True Story of the Royal House of Stewart and the Hidden Lineage of the Kings and Queens of Scotland,* Dorset, Boston: Element Books Ltd., 2000.

Osborn, Diane K. *Reflections on the Art of Living: A Joseph Campbell Companion,* New York: HarperPerennial, 1991.

Plowden, Alison. *The Young Elizabeth: The First Twenty-five Years of Elizabeth I,* London: Sutton Publishing Ltd., 1971.

Plowden, Alison. *Two Queens in One Isle: The Deadly Relationship of Elizabeth I and Mary Queen of Scots,* Sussex, England: The Harvester Press, 1984.

Rait, Robert S. and Annie I. Cameron. *King James's Secret: Negotiations Between Elizabeth I and James VI Relating to the Execution of Mary Queen of Scots, From the Warrender Papers,* London: Nisbet & Co., Ltd., 1927.

Richardson, Joanna. Charles Baudelaire: *Selected Poems,* Middlesex, England: Penguin Books Ltd., 1975.

Schaup, Suzanne. *Sophia: Aspects of the Divine Feminine Past and Present,* York Beach, Maine: Nicholas-Hays, Inc., 1997.

Tannahill, Reay. *Fatal Majesty,* New York: St. Martins Griffin, 1998.

Weber, Bernard Clarke. *The Youth of Mary Stuart, Queen of Scots,* Philadelphia: Dorrance and Company Publishers, 1941.

INDEX